Start with the Heart

Keys to Successful Living

John Wesley Hart

"Above all else, guard your heart, for everything you do flows from it."

Proverbs 4:23 (NIV)

Dedication

I have dedicated this book to Meg, my faithful wife, since 1983. She has persevered through trials, allowing God to work all things for good (Romans 8:28). To this day, I am amazed by her extravagant giving, thrifty spirit, contentment, respect for me, and her wonderful mother's heart. Meg is my best friend, my lover, and my partner in ministry.

CONTENTS

Acknowledgments

To Dave & Patti Heindel and Jason Fouts for their help in editing.

To Jeff Kline and Jean Blatchford for their marketing advice.

To Leslie McCallum for her prayers and encouragement to start a podcast.

To Pastor Phil McCallum, who wrote the foreword to this book.

To Owen and Ieleen Hart for their help in designing the Stewardship and Romance logo.

To Becky Omli, who led our first live women's group.

To Christian Peralta, Uila Lefiti, Jason Fouts, and Patti Fouts, our first online couples' group.

To Christian Johnson, Kyle Redzinak, Christian Peralta, and Chase Harrison, our first online men's group.

To my wife, Meg, for her continual encouragement and for creating this book's beautiful cover.

Foreword

You are holding a book in your hand. Let me recommend the couple behind the book—the Harts. Every Sunday, three rows from the front, I see the bright faces of John and Meg. I get to be their pastor. There are at least five reasons I recommend that you take this course. What are my five reasons? The proof of their success is in each of the five children they have raised. Each one is living life on purpose, married to a perfect match, and each one making a difference in the world with God.

What are John and Meg's trade secrets of successful living? You're holding the Hart codebook of success in your hands. This manual is not a book about marriage. Yet, these principles could prepare you as the answer to someone's prayers. Marriage is not always the right goal because the Bible tells us that singleness can be a great success if you let the Lord start with your heart.

I have watched broken relationships fracture, and I've also watched divisions between a man and woman heal. When a relationship is salvaged and renovated, it's usually because two very different people took time to work on themselves before upgrading the dynamics of their home. This book will help you to develop yourself, so in turn, you can benefit others.

Some of the most content humans I know are single. Perhaps your call of singleness is for a short time, or maybe for a lifetime. Maybe your single life is willing, or perhaps it's reluctant. When I've watched people happily flying solo in life, it's because they take to heart instructions like those in this book. This book is the manual on how to become successful in your heart and life. From these principles, your friendships, loves, community, and client relationships flow. Are you ready to become a success at heart? You need only to turn the next page and let the Harts speak into your heart.

Phil McCallum, Lead Pastor, Evergreen Church, Bothell, WA

Phil McCallum

Preface

God focuses on what is unseen. I Samuel 16:7 says, "For the Lord does not see as man sees; for man looks at the outward appearance, but the Lord looks at the *heart*." In the days that Jesus ministered here on earth, he noticed that many religious leaders had hearts that were in poor condition. He warned the people not to imitate these "leaders." Jesus continually underscored matters of the heart: "A good man out of the good treasure of his *heart* brings forth good, and an evil man out of the evil treasure of his *heart* brings forth evil. For out of the abundance of the *heart* his mouth speaks" (Luke 6:45). Read through the four Gospels and notice how many times Jesus changes the focus of the conversation to the condition of a person's heart. How many organizations emphasize the nurturing of the heart? Find one that does, and you will likely also find some spiritual health in that place. According to Psychology Today, "the average high school kid today has the same level of anxiety as the average psychiatric patient in the early 1950s." Today's youth are ripe for a revival of the heart.

Over the years, Meg and I have been talking about creating materials for young people who are interested in preparing for marriage and family. We started a podcast called "Stewardship and Romance". After recording nine episodes, we realized that young people needed more than just practical home, health, and money management hacks. They needed prepared hearts. We go to university to launch our careers, but how many of us study to become successful marriage partners, fathers, and mothers?

During the pandemic, I studied what the Bible had to say about the heart, focusing on thirty hot topics. This research became the backbone of our first online course, Start with the Heart: Keys to Successful Living. That is the purpose of this book--to teach you to become proactive in matters of the heart, to help you understand, own, and apply God's heart principles. As you begin to use these "keys" from God's Word, don't be surprised if you see some exciting changes. Of course, we are not suggesting that all your problems will go away as soon as you finish the course; but we are confident that you will see a progressive transformation in your life as you begin to apply these principles. Some of the changes will happen immediately, and others may take time. But just keep moving forward!

Remember, your heart is more like an oven than a microwave. It absorbs truth and changes over time. You'll discover that certain elements help your heart own the truth a little better: spoken prayer, writing, art, music, study, projects, and discussion. As you go through this course, take the time to look up the verses, complete the activities, and participate in discussions. For some lessons, you may even want to order and read a suggested book. As you continue this wholehearted approach, you may start noticing that, more and more, you are becoming free from things that have been weighing you down. You may also begin to see some progress in areas of your life where you've been stuck.

Remember, this curriculum is not intended to be the final and complete word on any given topic. It is simply a tool you can use to understand, own, and apply some of the timeless principles God has made available to us in his Word. These truths work because they emanate from Jesus Christ. In fact, Jesus is the truth! (John 14:6). We begin to walk in personal freedom, physical and emotional healing, and restored relationships to the extent that that we embrace his ways. No one understands us better than our loving Father. God has good plans for us. He wants us to succeed in life. Jeremiah 29:11 reads, "For I know the plans I have for you, declares the LORD, plans for welfare and not for evil, to give you a future and a hope."

Introduction

Why do we call this course "Start with the Heart"? Proverbs 4:23 (NIV) says, "My son, pay attention to what I say; turn your ear to my words. Do not let them out of your sight; keep them within your *heart*, for they are life to those who find them and health to one's whole body. Above all else, guard your *heart*, for everything you do flows from it." The heart is the control center, the seat of the will. For that reason, we must make every effort to guard it.

Here are a few guidelines to follow so that you get the most of this course:

Pace Yourself

In some areas, you may be able to digest the truth more quickly, but you may need to slow down and do some more in-depth study in others. Whatever pace you decide on, we recommend that you take enough time to absorb the truth at a deep level, practicing each principle. As Jesus said in Matthew 7, "Anyone who listens to my teaching and *follows it* is wise, like a person who builds a house on solid rock."

Find a Mentor

Just as every dedicated athlete in the natural has a coach, spiritual training also requires a mentor. Find a Godly person you trust who will encourage you to be all God has designed you to be.

Complete the Activities

- "Heart talks" (an introduction to a topic along with a personal story, Bible passages, and additional readings.)
- Meditations
- Discussion Questions
- Application steps ("Live it")

- Quizzes

Be part of a discussion group

Small group discussion is the best way to experience this course. You'll need a host who can also moderate each gathering. Ideally, when a group has completed the course, another group leader will start gearing up for a new session. The goal is ongoing discipleship.

Special Notes:

- All scripture references are from the English Standard Version (ESV) unless otherwise noted.
- This course provides only an introduction to each key, not a comprehensive study of each topic. Statements relating to the Bible are doctrinally correct to the best of the author's knowledge.
- Although this publication is designed to provide accurate information in regard to the subject matter covered, the publisher and the author assume no responsibility for errors, inaccuracies, omissions, or any other inconsistencies herein. This publication is not a substitute for direct expert assistance. If such a level of assistance is required, the services of a competent professional should be sought.

KEY 1
FIND FRIENDSHIP

Quote of the Day

"Friendship is born at the moment when one person says to another: 'What! You too? I thought I was the only one."
C.S. Lewis

Ever feel like you were the only one that felt lonely? You're in good company. Many people think the same way. They often mistakenly believe that everyone, except them, is enjoying "the good life" (whatever that is). But deep and lasting fulfillment is not found in popularity, fun times, food, drink, sex, hobbies, or achievement. These are all good when put in their proper place, but they are not a cure for loneliness. Deep and lasting friendship is a beautiful gift. Some friends are people we just met, acquaintances. Others are casual friends. Then there are those one or two who are close friends. What a treasure they are! A close friend is much more than someone who regularly "likes" your comments on social media. They are someone who would drop everything to be by your side if you were in trouble. They are someone you could talk to any time of the day or night—someone who listens to your heart, not just your words.

How to begin a friendship with God

Jesus wants a friendship with you. He is near you right now, standing at the door of your heart (Revelation 3:20). Christ paid the penalty for your sin on the cross, but you have a choice to make, a decision in your own heart. (Romans 10:9). Wherever you are right now, thank him for what he did for you on the cross, repent of your sins, and invite him into your heart. Here is a prayer that you could pray:

> *"Dear Father, thank you for loving me. I am sorry for my sins. Thank you for sending Jesus to pay the penalty for all my sin on the cross. I receive you now. Come into my heart and be the Lord of my life. Amen."*

If you prayed that prayer from your heart, you are now a child of God. Welcome to God's family! Your next step is to be baptized. You'll be learning about what that means in Key 24: Keep Covenant.

Meditate on it
Transforming the mind & emotions

Greater love has no one than this, that someone lay down his life for his friends.
John 15:13

1. Read it in context: John 15:12-17 (This will help you learn the true meaning of the verse.)
2. Say it out loud. (This starts the process of bringing the verse into your mind.)
3. Write it out. (As you write it, the Word is further impressed on your mind.)

_____

_____

_____

4. Pray it. (For example) "Jesus, thank you for laying down your life for me. Fill me with your unconditional love so that I can be a true friend." (This takes John 15:13 through your heart.)

5. Write down your prayer. (This takes it deeper into your heart and creates a repeatable record.)

_____

_____

_____

_____

Discuss it
Share your thoughts

1. In your opinion, what are the top qualities of a close friend?

2. Share about your relationship with a close friend. What made that relationship special?

3. How could you get closer to God as a friend?

Live it
Choose one or more activities, then write what happened

1. Talk to God every day as you would a close friend. Tell him everything--your joys and sorrows, your successes, and your failures.

2. If you don't already have a close friend, ask God to show you who you could reach out to. Then, if they are willing, make time to share with them regularly.

3. Remember to ask good questions and listen more than you talk.

_____

_____

_____

_____

_____

_____

_____

Recommended Reading

Here's a book related to this subject that will help you think differently about your relationships. It's called *The Power of Who* by Bob Beaudine. You'll be learning how to apply biblical principles of relationship.

Quiz
*True/False

1. ___ A close friend is someone who listens to your heart as well as your words.

2. ___ You can tell how many true friends you have through social media.

3. ___ An acquaintance will drop everything to be by your side if you are in trouble.

4. ___ God will remain your friend, even if you are dealing with sin in your life.

5. ___ We pray scripture back to God so that it will affect our hearts.

*Answers to quiz questions are in the back of the book.

KEY 2
ENJOY YOUR SPIRITUAL INHERITANCE

Quote of the Day

"Who are we? We are children of God. Our potential is unlimited.

Our inheritance is sacred."

Russell M. Nelson

You became a new creation when you prayed to receive Christ as your Lord and Savior (II Corinthians 5:17). As Jesus said, you were "born again" (John 3:3). Father God has adopted you, which means you are now part of his bloodline, honored as nobility, and legally entitled to all the rights and privileges of being a member of God's family. The angels marvel at this! Take ownership of your inheritance by declaring the truth in your own words:

Declare out loud:

- I am completely forgiven of all my past sins (Matthew 26:28), and I will apply the Blood of Jesus to any sins I commit in the future. (I John 1:7).
- I am free from fear of disapproval by God because he already approves of me because of what Christ accomplished for me. (Romans 8:15).

- I have the right to use the name of Jesus. (John 14:13). I have authority over the devil because I bear the family name (Mark 16:17).

- I can call God "Abba" (Daddy) because I am his child and can come to him in prayer with any request anytime (Romans 8:15).

- I am an heir of God with a glorious inheritance (Ephesians 1:19-23).

- God will make my suffering work for my good (Romans 8:28).

- Since I now live in God's favor (Psalm 84:11), I can claim his promises any time (II Peter 1:4).

- I am no longer a victim of my past because my new royal bloodline supersedes the old one (I Peter 2:9).

- After this life, I will live forever with God and my brothers and sisters in Christ for all eternity (John 3:16).

- I have the right to be free (John 8:36).

- I have peace with God (Romans 5:1-2), and I can live in peace at all times (John 14:27).

- I have been given the Holy Spirit as my comforter, teacher, helper, and advocate. He also has provided me with gifts with which I can be a source of tremendous blessing for others (I Corinthians 12:7-11).

This incredible inheritance has been made available to you so you can be a source of great blessing to others. (Read Ephesians 1:3-13.) As you read the Bible from cover to cover, watch how God looks for a people to honor so they can be a blessing to the world. Learn how to exercise what God has made available to you. It starts by hearing the Word, speaking it, then acting on it.

Meditate on it
Transforming the mind & emotions

Instead of your shame, you will receive a double portion, and instead of disgrace, you will rejoice in your inheritance. And so, you will inherit a double portion in your land, and everlasting joy will be yours.

Isaiah 61:7

1. Read it in context: Isaiah 61:5-7.
2. Say it out loud. Isaiah 61:7
3. Write it out.

_____

_____

_____

_____

4. Pray it: "Jesus, thank you for taking away all of my shame. I will now have a double portion. Instead of dishonor, I will rejoice in the great inheritance you have given me."
5. Write down your prayer.

_____

_____

_____

_____

_____

_____

_____

Discuss it
Share your thoughts

1. Do you believe God completely forgives you? Why do you think that?
2. Discuss your feelings about God's approval of you.
3. Talk about a time when you took authority over something in the name of Jesus.

Live it
Choose one or more activities, then write what happened

1. Repent of any known sin and put it under the Blood of Christ. "Lord Jesus, I repent for _____, and I now put that sin under the blood of Jesus. Thank you for forgiving me."
2. Keep your heart free from fear (Romans 8:15). "Father, thank you that I am no longer a slave to fear. I am your child."
3. Take authority using the name of Jesus. "In the name of Jesus, as a child of God, I take authority over a spirit of fear. Lord, your Word says you have not given us a spirit of fear but of power, love, and self-control (II Timothy 1:7).
4. Claim the promises of God. "Lord, thank you that you are going to work this situation for good according to your promise." (Romans 8:28).

_____

_____

_____

_____

_____

_____

_____

_____

_____

_____

_____

Quiz
True/False

1. ___ If you received Christ as your Lord and Savior, God considers you as nobility.

2. ___ We earn Father's love by doing good things.

3. ___ You must continue to work hard to keep God's approval.

4. ___ Jesus promised that we could be free from shame.

5. ___ The gifts Holy Spirit gives you are a source of blessing to others.

KEY 3
FOLLOW THE RIGHT PATH

Quote of the Day

"Not until we have become humble and teachable, standing in awe of God's holiness and sovereignty, acknowledging our own littleness, distrusting our own thoughts, and willing to have our minds turned upside down, can divine wisdom become ours."

J.I. Packer

When we say the word "wisdom," we often think of Solomon. I Kings 3:3-14 says, "Solomon loved the Lord, walking in the statutes of David, his father." The Lord came to him in a dream to reward him for following in his father David's footsteps. David was "a man after God's own heart." God loved him so much that he continued to bless his descendants. Jesus was in the lineage of David, and since you are now in God's family, you are too!

Scripture says Solomon could have asked for long life, riches, or the life of his enemies, but he asked for wisdom. God was so impressed that he gave Solomon the wisdom he prayed for and several other things he did not ask for. As a result, Solomon became the wisest and richest man on earth. This story clearly shows us God's priorities. He values wisdom above anything else because he knows if we get wisdom, then everything else we need will fall into place as it should. God wants us to come to him asking for what is closest to his heart, for eternal treasure. As we do that, he generously supplies us with the temporal things we need too. In Matthew 6:33, Jesus said, ". . .but seek first his kingdom and his righteousness, and all these things will be given to you as well."

What is wisdom? First, we need to remember—wisdom and knowledge are different. Knowledge is what we know, something acquired through study, but wisdom is seeing and responding to knowledge from God's perspective. In other words, wisdom is all about carrying God's heart—which starts with being teachable. That is the purpose of this course, to help you see life from God's perspective and apply it. God knows the path you should take. If you're walking through some doubts right now about which way to go, stop and ask for directions. James 1:5 says, "If any of you lacks wisdom, let him ask God, who gives generously to all without reproach, and it will be given him." So come to your heavenly Father in prayer every day, asking for wisdom first. Make it your priority to get God's perspective.

Meditate on it
Transforming the mind & emotions

If any of you lacks wisdom, let him ask God, who gives generously to all without reproach, and it will be given him.

James 1:5

1. Read it in context: James 1:5-8
2. Say it out loud. James 1:5
3. Write it out:

_____

_____

_____

_____

_____

4. Pray it: "Father, thank you for always being so generous. You promised me wisdom whenever I need it, so I'm asking for it now, believing I have received it."

5. Write down your prayer:

_____

_____

_____

_____

_____

_____

_____

_____

Discuss it

Share your thoughts

1. What is the difference between knowledge and wisdom?

2. Describe someone you know who is truly wise (besides Jesus).

3. How will you grow in wisdom this week?

Live it

1. Read or listen to God's Word daily.

2. Listen to Godly teaching at your church.

3. Listen to Bible-based podcasts or radio shows.

4. Read books that help you grow in your faith.

_____

_____

_____

_____

_____

_____

_____

_____

_____

_____

_____

Quiz
True/False

1. ___ To gain wisdom, we must first be teachable.

2. ___ A wise person sees from God's perspective.

3. ___ Some people were just born wise.

4. ___ Wisdom and knowledge are pretty much the same.

5. ___ The best way to get more wisdom is by learning lots of facts.

KEY 4
GROW IN CONFIDENCE

Quote of the Day

"Faith never knows where it is being led,

but it loves and knows the One who is leading."

Oswald Chambers

As believers, each of us has been given a different measure of faith as a gift from God. Romans 12:3 says, "For by the grace given to me, I say to everyone among you not to think of himself more highly than he ought to think, but to think with sober judgment, each according to the measure of faith that God has assigned."

Faith needs exercise! As we make daily choices to trust the Holy Spirit and obey his voice, we grow in confidence as sons and daughters of God. Remember—our surety is not in ourselves. It is in the Lord. It is not self-confidence but God-confidence. As always, Jesus is our example. He consistently spoke of his relationship with his Father and did nothing apart from him. That is how he wants us to live, confident because of our relationship to Father God.

We will not have to wait long before another opportunity to exercise our "faith muscles." Fear will present itself. But when it does, here is what we do: Psalm 56:4 says, "When I am afraid, in you I place my trust." Vocalize your trust in God. When it comes to fear, the battle is within us.

Though we cannot control what is happening around us, we can exercise our faith and gain confidence on the inside.

Fear is "false evidence appearing real"—an imagining. We all have experienced tremendous anxiety at different points in our lives, especially when losing income, health, or those we love. But victory over fear does not rest in suppressing it, but in changing our focus. The next time you start to feel fearful, don't condemn yourself. Just take a deep breath, tell God your feelings, then lift your voice and agree with his promises. As you regularly do this, you will find your confidence growing.

There are many examples of faith workouts in Scripture. Read the story of Ananias in Acts 9:10-19. Ananias had every reason to be fearful when the Lord instructed him to minister to Saul (the man imprisoning and killing Christians). Nevertheless, he exercised the faith he had been given and was able to follow through with what the Lord told him to do. How confident are you in the Lord? Are you convinced God is good and that he always keeps his promises? Take time today to exercise your faith, declaring that your trust is in the Lord.

Fearproof

If you need some extra instruction and support in overcoming fear, our friend, J.R., has produced something powerful that will help you overcome it. *Fearproof by JR Covey* is a six-week course designed to help identify, isolate, and overcome fear through faith, wisdom, and work.

Meditate on it
Transforming the mind & emotions

Trust in the Lord with all your heart, and do not lean on your own understanding. In all your ways, acknowledge him, and he will make straight your paths.

Proverbs 3:5-6

1. Read it in context: Proverbs 3:5-8
2. Say it out loud. Proverbs 3:5-6
3. Write it out:

_____

_____

_____

_____

_____

4. Pray it: "Lord, I trust you now with all my heart. I will not lean on my own understanding. In this situation, I know you are near me, and you are making my paths straight."
5. Write down your prayer:

_____

_____

_____

_____

_____

_____

_____

_____

_____

Discuss it
Share your thoughts

1. Who is someone you are aware of who lives by faith and not by fear? How do you think they got there?

2. Describe something you have done in the past that has helped you grow in confidence.

3. What could you do this week that would deal a blow to your fears?

Live it
Choose one or more activities, then write what happened

1. Tell God (out loud) that you trust him. "I trust you, Father with _____."

2. Call to mind a time when God brought you through a storm. (Write it in your journal and share it with a friend.)

3. Sing along with songs about trusting God.

4. Be still and wait in the Lord's presence. Write down any verses or thoughts the Holy Spirit brings to your mind in your journal.

5. Write down the promises of God you need to cling to and pray them to God daily. Example: "Lord, thank you for supplying all my needs, according to your riches in glory."

_____

_____

_____

_____

_____

_____

_____

_____

_____

_____

_____

_____

_____

_____

_____

_____

Quiz
True/False

1. ___ A good definition of fear is: "false evidence appearing real."

2. ___ The best way to overcome fear is to keep pushing it back down.

3. ___ Our faith needs exercise to grow.

4. ___ We can cultivate trust by calling to mind the times God carried us through.

5. ___ Claiming the promises of God helps us overcome fear.

KEY 5
HOLD ON TO YOUR JOY

Quote of the Day

The joy of the Lord will arm us against the assaults of our spiritual enemies and put our mouths out of taste for those pleasures with which the tempter baits his hooks.

Matthew Henry

Are happiness and joy just two different words for the same thing? No, happiness and joy are different. Happiness starts on the outside and works its way in; whereas joy begins on the inside and works its way out. Happiness depends upon what happens, such as getting something you want or achieving a goal. But joy grows as a fruit of the Spirit (Galatians 5:22-23) and has nothing to do with your present circumstances.

Joy is the primary indicator that you have been with Jesus and that you are abiding in him (John 15:4). In that verse, the word "abide" means "to rest; to continue; to stand firm; to dwell." For a branch, it means to stay connected to the vine. Joy is like Wi-fi. When you are connected to Christ, his life flows through you. You can tell when you have become disconnected from Christ, and so can everyone else! When you sense a lack of joy, check your connection to Christ. By the way-- if you lack joy, that does not mean God is mad at you or does not love you anymore. It just means that it's time to reconnect!

Joseph (Genesis 37-47) is well-known for his many gifts and his determination to live in the fear of the Lord. Though not explicitly stated, Joseph's story seems to imply that he learned to choose joy during very difficult circumstances. (Psalm 112:1 says, "Praise the Lord! How *joyful* are those who fear the Lord and delight in obeying his commands.") The fear of the Lord and joy go hand-in-hand. Though Joseph's brothers threw him in a pit and sold him as a slave to Egypt, he learned to be productive regardless of his circumstances. At one point, he was falsely accused of sexual harassment and sent to the dungeon. But even there, others were drawn to him. The captain of the guard noticed Joseph and put him in charge. Then after his release from prison, Pharaoh gave him authority over all of Egypt!

Yes, there will be times of pain and sorrow, but God does not want us to cave in and quit during those times. He has in mind that we get up again, dust off, and refocus. Just like Joseph, we can be productive—even if we've hit rock bottom. But how do we get there? It's by drinking from the right source—Jesus himself (John 4:7-15). Each day we are presented with an opportunity to refuse to drink from bitterness and discouragement—and instead, drink from the great, refreshing well of the Holy Spirit.

Meditate on it
Transforming the mind & emotions

Abide in my love. If you keep my commandments, you will abide in my love, just as I have kept my Father's commandments and abide in his love. These things I have spoken to you, that my joy may be in you, and that your joy may be full.

John 15:9-11

1. Read it in context: John 15:1-11

2. Say it out loud. John 15:9-11

3. Write it out:

_____

_____

_____

_____

_____

_____

4. Pray it: "Jesus, I want to be close to you today. Show me if there is anything that is hindering our relationship together. I give you my heart, and I purpose to closely follow your Word so that I can stay full of your joy."

5. Write down your prayer:

_____

_____

_____

_____

_____

_____

_____

_____

Discuss it
Share your thoughts

1. Who are the most joyful people that you know? What makes them so joyful?

2. Would most people that know you describe you as a joyful person? Why is that?

3. What steps could you take this week to start living in more joy?

Live it
Choose one or more activities, then write what happened

1. Gain a clear conscience by asking for forgiveness for any known sin, then make any needed restitution. (I John 1:9; Matthew 5:23-24)

2. Thank God for what you *do* have every day.

3. Do at least one random act of kindness every day.

4. Do something you enjoy with at least one other like-minded person.

5. Ask God to fill you with His joy!

_____

_____

_____

_____

_____

_____

_____

_____

_____

Quiz
True/False

1. ___ Joy and happiness are pretty much the same.

2. ___ Joy grows as the result of a love relationship with Jesus.

3. ___ We abide in Christ by keeping his commandments.

4. ___ One way to cultivate joy is by maintaining an attitude of thankfulness.

5. ___ There is nothing you can do to help your soul find joy.

KEY 6
BE MEEK, NOT WEAK

Quote of the Day

"The man who has no opinion of himself at all can never be hurt if others do not acknowledge him. Hence, be meek. He who is without expectation cannot fret if nothing comes to him. It is self-evident that these things are so. The lowly man and the meek man are really above all other men, above all other things."

Henry Drummond

Guess which film is likely the most-watched motion picture of all time. According to the New York Times, it's the 1979 Jesus movie, viewed more than six billion times! Why so many views of this particular movie? Perhaps people were drawn by the meekness of Jesus portrayed in the film. Though Jesus was (and is) Almighty God incarnate, he used his power to bring healing and freedom to others. Strength under control is impressive to watch.

Meekness is not weakness; it's relaxed confidence. In God's way of thinking, it's when you are secure enough in who you are that you no longer focus on yourself but on others. No one was more focused on others than Jesus. He was so confident in his relationship with his Father that his enemies could never get under his skin.

Meekness is a posture of the heart that says, "I make your needs my priority." Jesus considered himself a servant, and he expects us to have the same attitude. In John chapter 13, he said to his disciples, "Whoever would be first among you must be your slave, even as the Son of Man came not to be served but to serve, and to give his life as a ransom for many."

The Scriptures are clear that great blessing is in store for the meek. In the sermon on the mount, Jesus said, Blessed, are the meek, for they shall inherit the earth." God exalts those who honor him. He promotes those who bear with the failings of others and choose not to react in anger. He lifts those who are gentle and treat others with patience, understanding, and respect, whether they deserve it or not.

What does a meek person look like today? It looks like a student who cares enough to help a classmate that no one else pays any attention to. It looks like a worker who faithfully serves, whether they get noticed or not. Most people tend to be repelled by individuals who are full of themselves but attracted to those who sacrificially give of themselves to others.

Besides Jesus, Moses was a notable example of meekness. Numbers 12:3 says, "Now the man Moses was very meek, more than all people who were on the face of the earth." What a statement! God chose Moses to lead an entire nation because of his meekness. Moses did not always agree with God, but he acknowledged and obeyed him. Meek people follow directions well. They are leadership material!

Meekness should be one of the top criteria for leadership because the meek person has strength that is under control. They are not going to react, do something impulsive, and hurt the organization. No, they will look at all the facts, pay attention to the needs of others, and make a decision that is in line with the company's vision. So, remember--meekness is not weakness; it's strength under control, and it's all about focusing on the needs of those around you every day.

Meditate on it
Transforming the mind & emotions

Humble yourselves, therefore, under God's mighty hand, that he may lift you up in due time. Cast all your anxiety on him because he cares for you.

I Peter 5:6-7

1. Read it in context: I Peter 5:6-11
2. Say it out loud. I Peter 5:6-7
3. Write it out:

_____

_____

_____

_____

_____

_____

_____

4. Pray it: "Father, I submit my will to you. You know better than I do what is best for me and what the right timing is. Have your way in me and through me today. I cast my anxiety on you because I know you love me."
5. Write down your prayer:

_____

_____

_____

_____

_____

_____

Discuss it

Share your thoughts

1. How would you define meekness?

2. Describe someone you know who is very meek.

3. Why do you think God chooses meek people to be leaders?

Live it

Choose one or more activities, then write what happened

1. Pray before posting something on social media that you might later regret.

2. Ask for God's help before making a decision.

3. Rather than react when confronted, pray before you respond.

4. Use gentle body language.

5. Practice meekness towards yourself. Don't fret over your imperfections.

6. Respond gently. "A gentle answer turns away wrath, but a harsh word stirs up anger", Proverbs 15:1

Quiz
True/False

1. ____ Meekness means putting yourself down.

2. ____ A genuinely meek person focuses more on others because he is secure in who he is.

3. ____ A meek person is often a miserable person.

4. ____ There are many blessings in store for the meek.

5. ____ A meek person delights in the Lord rather than boasting in his accomplishments.

KEY 7
ACTIVATE BLESSINGS

Quote of the Day

"God didn't add another day to your life because you needed it. He did it because someone out there needs you!"

Unknown

Spoken blessings are life-giving words that can encourage, protect, bring healing, and release God's favor. **Proverbs 25:11** says, "A word aptly spoken is like apples of gold in settings of silver." As you go through your week, be watching for opportunities the Holy Spirit gives you to bless someone. It can be as simple as a sincere compliment or a written note.

Hebrews 3:13 says, "But encourage one another day after day, as long as it is still called "Today," so that none of you will be hardened by the deceitfulness of sin." Yes, consistent words of blessing help those who are struggling with sinful habits. (One reason they are they are addicted, at least partially, is because they missed out on being blessed.) We also need to learn how to bless our enemies. In Matthew 5, Jesus said, "But I say to you, love your enemies, bless those who curse you, do good to those who hate you, and pray for those who spitefully use you and persecute you." And in **Romans 12:14,** Paul wrote, "Bless those who persecute you; bless and do not curse."

Then there is another type of blessing where someone of significance in your life speaks words that result in a turning point in your life or outstanding achievement, such as the beginning of a new career. The individual who expressed the blessing may not even be aware they were speaking one, but the words had a powerful impact.

One interesting fact about blessings is - the one being blessed may not even know he is being blessed! For example, Jesus blessed infants -- and who knows what good things took place in each of their lives as a result! We spoke words of blessing over each of our five children as we put them to bed at night -- and we know that made a difference for them. By the way--the most accessible people to bless on the planet are children. The reason why is because they are generally uncomplicated and are more inclined to believe. They just take God at his Word! In Mark 10, Jesus said, "Let the children come to me; do not hinder them, for to such belongs the kingdom of God . . . whoever does not receive the kingdom of God like a child shall not enter it. . . and he took them in his arms and blessed them, laying his hands on them."

Jesus instructed his disciples to bless the atmosphere of people's homes. In Luke 10:5-6, he said, "But whatever house you enter, first say, 'Peace to this house.' And if the son of peace is there, your peace will rest on it; if not, it will return to you."

If you want to give someone (or a group of people) a significant blessing, then use Scripture itself to compose it before you speak it over them. Here's an example of a blessing we crafted from Numbers 6:24-26: "May the Lord God bless you and keep you from the torments of fear and anxiety. May He cause His face to shine upon you with His power and love, and may He give you a sound mind. Through His perfect love, may God give you the grace to cast out fear. May He lift up His countenance upon you with freedom as you tell Him every detail of your need in earnest, thankful prayer, and may He give you His peace that surpasses all understanding as He keeps your heart and mind safe through Jesus Christ."

Consider writing a blessing for someone, speaking it over them, then giving them what you wrote. Meg and I did that for each of our children when they reached twelve or so. We invited family and friends to come to our home, served food, and then had a special time of blessing for one of our children. The blessing was written down so they could always have it. Today -

why not ask the Lord who you could bless, then just do it! Here are some ideas that you could incorporate into "Live it" below. If you would like even more ideas like this, check out this this powerful little book called, "Prayers that Activate Blessing" by John Eckhardt.

Meditate on it
Transforming the mind & emotions

Do not repay evil for evil or reviling for reviling, but on the contrary, bless, for to this you were called, that you may obtain a blessing.

I Peter 3:9

1. Read it in context: I Peter 3:8-10
2. Say it out loud: I Peter 3:9
3. Write it out.

_____

_____

_____

_____

_____

_____

_____

4. Pray it: "Lord, I will not repay evil for evil or insult others when they insult me, but bring to mind ways I can instead bless others even when they don't deserve it—just as you continually bless me when I don't deserve it."
5. Write down your prayer.

Discuss it
Share your thoughts

1. Tell about a time that someone shared with you an encouraging word that ended up changing your life.
2. Who could you bless? How would you do that?

Live it
Choose one or more activities, then write what happened

1. Pray for the revelation of someone's true identity in Christ.
2. Be attentive to the true needs that someone is experiencing.
3. Write little notes to the ones you love.
4. Call a friend on the phone just to talk.
5. Take a moment to listen to the story of an older person.
6. Speak encouraging words from your heart to those around you.
7. If you are married, speak about how wonderful your spouse is in front of others.
8. Use Scripture to formulate a spoken blessing over someone's life.

Quiz
True/False

1. ___ A blessing can release the favor of God on a person.

2. ___ Words can create but also destroy.

3. ___ You have to wait until someone is 12 years old to give them a blessing.

4. ___ Even a little note can be a blessing.

5. ___ Only a priest can give a blessing.

KEY 8
TAKE A WALK IN THEIR SHOES

Quote of the Day

"Empathy is patiently and sincerely seeing the world through the other person's eyes. It is not learned in school; it is cultivated over a lifetime."

Albert Einstein

Empathy is the ability to understand what someone is going through, even imagining what they might be thinking or feeling. Of course, it is easier to empathize with someone if you have experienced a comparable situation yourself. But all of us can learn to empathize.

Jesus is the embodiment of empathy. He profoundly understands our pain because he created us and knows our every thought. In **Psalm 139:4**, the psalmist says, "Before a word is on my tongue you, Lord, know it completely." Jesus knows and understands what we are feeling. He proved his love for us by walking in our shoes. He voluntarily left the beauty of heaven and take on human form, but he became one of us so that we would know how much he understands what we go through. **Hebrews 4:15** says, "For we do not have a high priest who is unable to empathize with our weaknesses, but we have one who has been tempted in every way just as we are, yet he did not sin."

Jesus invites us to soak in his empathy, then pay it forward. As it says in I John 4:19, "We love because he first loved us." Empathy is a quality that is available to each of us because the Spirit of God lives within us. All that is required is that we choose his mindset.

Philippians 2:5-8 says, "Have this mind among yourselves, which is yours in Christ Jesus, who, though he was in the form of God, did not count equality with God a thing to be grasped, but emptied himself, by taking the form of a servant, being born in the likeness of men. And being found in human form, he humbled himself by becoming obedient to the point of death, even death on a cross." Notice how the verse begins: "Have this mind among yourselves." As his beloved children, Father calls us to set aside anything we are grasping for and focus on serving others. And the best way to do that is to first empathize with the ones we are serving.

For some fine examples of this in modern times, study the lives of missionaries like Jim Elliott, Mary Slessor, Gladys Aylward, and CT Studd. These were all normal human beings like you and me who left the comfort of their own homes and identified with the people they were serving by living among them—"walking in their shoes."

We would likely find that many problems in today's society could be solved simply by beginning with empathy. Each of us is a soldier in God's army of love, commissioned for compassion. Instead of hating, we love. Instead of judging, we show mercy. And instead of only looking out for our interests, we look out for the interests of others. As it says in Philippians 2:3-4, "Do nothing out of selfish ambition or vain conceit. Rather, in humility, value others above yourselves, not looking to your own interests but each of you to the interests of the others."

Jesus always looked to the interests of others. He understood how they arrived at their present condition, and he loved them as they were, understanding their pain and listening to their stories. Why did he do this? To set an example for us! He wants us to learn how to give people a leg up when they are struggling. Remember that empathizing with someone does not mean we condone their sin; no, it paves the way for them to overcome. The woman caught in adultery (in John 8) and the woman at the well with a shameful past (John 4) had one thing in common; they both overcame because they were treated with compassion and respect by the Savior. The words Jesus used were, "Neither do I condemn you. Go and sin no more."

So, let's learn to empathize with one another, even in small ways. Let's give each other a little more patience, a bit of understanding, and a bit more space to make mistakes. For most of us, that's all we need to move ahead when we feel stuck. When we know someone else understands what we are experiencing, it often gives us that extra boost we need to get up and get going again. As it says in Ephesians 4:2, ". . . with all humility and gentleness, with patience, bearing with one another in love."

Meditate on it

Transforming the mind & emotions

Rejoice with those who rejoice, weep with those who weep.

Romans 12:15

1. Read it in context: Romans 12:14-21
2. Say it out loud: Romans 12:15
3. Write it out:

_____

_____

_____

_____

_____

_____

4. Pray it: (Example) "Lord, give me a heart that understands people and can empathize with them, weeping when they weep, and rejoicing when they rejoice. Root out of me an inconsiderate spirit and fill me with your unconditional love."

5. Write down your prayer:

_____   _____

_____

_____

_____

_____

_____

_____

_____

Discuss it

Share your thoughts

1. Tell about a time someone empathized with you. How did it make you feel?

2. How can someone know that you are genuinely empathizing with them?

3. Share some practical ways that you could express empathy to those close to you.

Live it

Choose one or more activities, then write what happened.

1. Look for opportunities to show understanding to people with messy lives. Practice listening.

2. Be comfortable with silence in a conversation when someone isn't sure of what to say.

3. Validate another person's emotions. Cry with them. Laugh with them.

4. Paraphrase what someone is saying, so they know you understand.

5. As the Holy Spirit directs, give to someone who is in need.

_____

_____

_____

_____

_____

_____

_____

_____

Quiz
True/False

1. ___ Empathy is the same thing as sympathy.

2. ___ Empathy is a mindset for us to choose.

3. ___ Empathy is only about weeping with those who weep.

4. ___ God can set you free from apathy.

5. ___ One way to cultivate empathy is to paraphrase the comment of a hurting person.

KEY 9
COMMIT TO PURITY

Quote of the Day

"The pursuit of purity is not about the suppression of lust, but about the reorientation of one's life to a larger goal."

Dietrich Bonhoeffer

In I Timothy 5, Paul is teaching his spiritual son, Timothy, about how to relate to people of all ages and genders: "Treat younger men as brothers, older women as mothers, and younger women as sisters, with absolute purity." Let's focus in on "treat younger women as sisters." How can a young man walk out this admonition? It seems like an impossible standard. But Jesus himself said, "Blessed are the pure in heart, for they will see God." (Matthew 5:8). To the extent that our hearts are pure, we experience God. Conversely, to the extent we entertain impure thoughts, our relationship with Jesus suffers, and as a result, so does our relationship with others.

Purity makes us attractive to the right people. When it comes to finding a spouse, looks are important, but being pure in heart is even more critical. Ladies, if you can tell that all a guy is interested in is getting you into bed—run the other direction! His heart is in the wrong place. A boy like this has the caboose in front of the engine. Wait for God's best! We live in a sex-crazed society that has everything backward. Many young adults these days consider sex as a past time, something we do together just for fun. But I Corinthians 6.16 says that when we have sex with someone, we become "one flesh" with them; it's a union of spirit, soul, and body. We often refer to this as a "soul tie," which is a subconscious emotional bond. Euphoria often comes initially, but eventually, one person loses interest or finds someone else they like better.

At the end of the day, we must view sex from God's perspective. He never intended we form union after union with multiple partners. For our protection and well-being, God wants us to enjoy sex only within covenant marriage. There is plenty of support for this in God's Word. Here are a few scriptures for you to look up and study on your own: Genesis 2:24; Hebrews 13:4; I Thessalonians 5:3-5; I Corinthians 6:18-20; I Corinthians 7:2,9.

When we follow Father God's plan for sex, we thrive; but when we sexually gratify ourselves before marriage, we end up hurting ourselves and those around us. Imagine this for a moment. What would the world be like if a much greater number of couples waited to have sex until the proper time? It would probably be a world of fewer broken hearts, less sexually transmitted diseases, fewer teen pregnancies, fewer unwanted pregnancies, fewer abortions, and less divorce (since marital breakups are often the result of mistrust and infidelity.) By the way— studies show that couples who cohabitate before marriage are much more likely to divorce after getting married.

Society has normalized premarital sex, but just because many people believe something is right does not make it right. Historically, human beings have never prospered by inventing truth. Though we live in an imperfect world, but God, in His mercy, reveals his ways to us. When we follow his instructions for life, we prosper, but we suffer when we reject what he says. One question a single might ask is: "OK, I understand premarital sex is a sin, but what do I do, then, with all my sexual desire?

Here are three guiding principles:

1. **Focus on building up your spirit.** When your regenerated spirit is in charge, then your soul and body will fall in line. When it's the other way around, you become a slave to your appetites. Don't focus on suppressing lust; focus on re-orienting to a larger goal.

2. **Keep listening to your conscience.** (I Timothy 4:1-2). Do not ignore those warnings on the dashboard of your soul. Martin Luther once said, "To violate conscience is neither right nor safe."

3. **Don't put yourself in a situation where you know you could fall morally.** Why? Because one little compromise can lead to another, then another. It is human nature. The mind loves to justify what the heart has chosen. So don't even get started with testing the limits of your self-control!

A single might ask: What do I do when I'm tempted sexually? I Corinthians 6:18 says, "Flee from sexual immorality. Every other sin a person commits is outside the body, but the sexually immoral person sins against his own body." The keyword in that verse is "flee." Don't think for a moment, "Oh, I can handle it. It's no big deal." Remember, wisdom is all about having God's perspective on a matter. Let's take a lesson from three men in the Bible who experienced sexual temptation: Joseph, Sampson, and David:

Consider Joseph. Potiphar's wife seduced him (Genesis 30), but Joseph embraced the way of wisdom. Joseph saw how giving in would hurt his master, his entire household, and his own life—so he chose the wisest course of action—he fled! That was the manly thing to do. In the end, God rewarded him by promoting him to be the ruler of the land, second only to Pharaoh.

Then, there's Sampson in the book of Judges. Even though there was no match for him, physically, Sampson's undoing was his fleshly lusts. Nevertheless, in the end, he did choose the way of wisdom by asking God for mercy and one more opportunity to defeat the Philistines—which he did.

Lastly, there was King David in II Samuel. He loved God intensely and was more courageous as a young man than any soldier on the battlefield, but there came a season in his life when he let his guard down and succumbed to lust and deceit. Nevertheless, he is still known as a man after God's own heart. Like Sampson, he cried out to God for mercy: "Create in me a clean heart, O God, and renew a right spirit within me." (Psalm 51).

It's wonderful to know that, even when we fall, God is merciful and is always there to pick us up and get us back on the main road again. If you've made some mistakes in your past in the area of purity, ask God to forgive you and cleanse you. If you have defrauded someone else, ask for their forgiveness. Then put it behind you. Do not condemn yourself. God is not scolding you. If you have been facing some sexual temptation, do what you can to get out of its path. If you are into porn on the internet, repent! Make every possible effort to stop, and then ask someone who genuinely cares about your welfare to hold you accountable. Do not try conquering this addiction alone! Most importantly, fill up on the love of Jesus every day! When you are full of him, you'll stay pure in heart.

Meditate on it
Transforming the mind & emotions

Since we have these promises, beloved, let us cleanse ourselves from every defilement of body and spirit, bringing holiness to completion in the fear of God.

II Corinthians 7:1

1. Read it in context: II Corinthians 6:15 – 7:1
2. Say it out loud. II Corinthians 7:1
3. Write it out:

_____

_____

_____

_____

_____

_____

_____

_____

4. **Pray it. (Example)** "Father, since I am yours, and you've promised to always be with me, I will cleanse myself from those things that bring defilement to my body and spirit, bringing my holiness to completion as I continue to live in your presence."

5. Write down your prayer.

_____

_____

_____

_____

_____

_____

_____

_____

Discuss it

Share your thoughts

1. What do you think this verse means, "Blessed are the pure in heart for they shall see God?"

2. What does it look like for a man to treat a young woman as a sister?

3. Talk about the dangers of premarital relationships.

4. Besides chastity, how else can a believer live in purity?

Live it

Choose one or more activities, then write what happened.

1. Ask God to forgive and cleanse you from any impure thoughts or actions.

2. Ask individuals for forgiveness if your past actions compromised them.

3. Abstain from lustful activities, such as pornography and other sexually explicit media.

4. Avoid situations that could lead to moral compromise, "take every thought captive" (II Corinthians 10:5) by refocusing on noble thoughts and activities (Philippians 4.8).

5. Flee from sexual temptation.

6. Find a Godly mentor with whom you can share your thoughts regularly.

7. Fill up daily on the Word of God and prayer.

_____

_____

_____

_____

_____

Quiz
True/False

1.___ Purity is all about suppressing lustful desires.

2.___ The biblical response to sexual temptation is to flee!

3.___ When it comes to moral purity, everyone should just do what they think is right for them.

4.___ King David was the only one in the Bible who got it right regarding purity.

5.___ One way to cultivate moral purity is by avoiding situations that could lead to compromise.

KEY 10
SUMMON YOUR COURAGE

Quote of the Day

"Christian courage is the willingness to say and do the right thing regardless of the earthly cost."

John Piper

How would you define courage? Courage in God's Kingdom means hearing a word from God, then acting on that word regardless. Webster's 1828 dictionary says courage is "that quality of mind which enables men to encounter danger and difficulties with firmness."

Courage is a must for the men and women in the military, but it is also an essential quality for each one of us in the trenches of day-to-day life. Bullied students need courage. Singles who desire marriage need courage when no life partner appears to be on the horizon. Couples need courage when they experience seasons of marital unrest. Parents need courage when their children experience growing pains and when their elderly parents need additional care.

Many narratives of courage in the Bible help us understand what it looks like—stories about courageous people like Abraham, Moses, Gideon, and David. One we especially like in the New Testament is the story of Peter walking on water: In Matthew 14, it says, "Immediately Jesus made the disciples get into the boat and go on ahead of him to the other side, while he dismissed the crowd. After he had dismissed them, he went up on a mountainside by himself to pray. Later that night, he was there alone, and the boat was already a considerable distance from land, buffeted by the waves because the wind was against it. Shortly before dawn, Jesus went out to them, walking on the lake. When the disciples saw him walking on the lake, they were terrified. 'It's a ghost,' they said and cried out in fear. But Jesus immediately said to them: 'Take courage! It is I. Don't be afraid.' 'Lord, if it's you,' Peter replied, 'tell me to come to you on the water. 'Come,' he said. Then Peter got down out of the boat, walked on water, and came toward Jesus. But when he saw the wind, he was afraid and, beginning to sink, cried out, 'Lord, save me!' Immediately Jesus reached out his hand and caught him. 'You of little faith,' he said, 'why did you doubt?' And when they climbed into the boat, the wind died down. Then those in the boat worshiped him, saying, 'Truly you are the Son of God.'"

From this story, we learn about the dynamics of courage. First, we discover that courage is something we *take* based on what Jesus has said. In the account of Peter walking on water, Jesus said to all the disciples, "Take courage! It is I. Don't be afraid." Only Peter took the Lord's direction to another level. All he needed from Jesus was an invitation—and he got one! That one word, "come," offered specifically to him, was the spark that ignited a fire of courage. Another thing we learn from the story is that courage can wane whenever we entertain doubt. Before Peter had finished his walk to Jesus, he began entertaining doubts, which diminished his faith. Hebrews 11:6 says, "Without faith, it is impossible to please God." Doubt reduces faith, breeding discouragement. The reason we get discouraged sometimes is due to rehearsing doubts instead of God's promises. It takes daily practice to fix our minds on Christ and his Word instead of ourselves and the thoughts of our natural mind.

What is Jesus saying to you? Is there a promise from God's Word that the Holy Spirit keeps bringing to your mind? As soon as you lock in on what God is saying, start moving! We love those movies where the hero in the story goes through an intense struggle, almost giving up hope, but suddenly remembers something told to them in childhood. A new fierceness comes into their eyes, their body fills with strength, and they do what most would think is impossible! As children of God, all we need to do is remember the words of Jesus, then rise in the power of the Spirit and accomplish it. If it's Jesus asking you to do it, you can do it!

Ready to build up some courage? Courage is developed by taking steps. It grows as we exercise our God-given freedom to choose. Humans are eternal beings made in the image of God. As part of that image, we can choose. God can help us make difficult choices. He wants us to learn to trust him and take some steps of faith. He gives us all the strength we need, then he asks us to go for a faith walk—to exercise our faith. Eagles instinctively know this universal principle. They push their eaglets out of the nest so that they will learn to fly. Resist the lie that says, "I can't do it! I know I'm going to fall! Replace that thought with God's truth "I can do all things through Christ who strengthens me!" The most often repeated command in the Bible—stated over 200 times—is do not fear.

Meditate on it

Transforming the mind & emotions

Have I not commanded you? Be strong and courageous. Do not be afraid; do not be discouraged, for the LORD your God will be with you wherever you go.

Joshua 1:9

1. Read it in context: Joshua 1:1-9

2. Say it out loud: Joshua 1:9

3. Write it out:

_____

_____

_____

_____

_____
_____
_____
_____

4. Pray it. (Example) "Lord, thank you for the strength you have given me for this moment. I will not be afraid or discouraged because you are with me right now."

5. Write down your prayer:

_____
_____
_____
_____
_____
_____
_____
_____
_____
_____

Discuss it

Share your thoughts

1. How would you define courage?

2. What is the most courageous thing you have ever done?

3. How will your courage grow?

Live it

Choose one or more activities, then write what happened.

1. Keep a journal of the good things God has done in your life.
2. Study the lives of people who have taken courage, such as Moses, Gideon, and David.
3. Respond quickly to the Holy Spirit's leadings.
4. Decide on a big goal, then take little steps to accomplish it.
5. Try something you've never done before.
6. Do something that used to make you fearful.
7. Praise others who are being courageous.
8. Listen to songs that feed your courage.

_____

_____

_____

_____

_____

_____

_____

_____

_____

_____

_____

Quiz
True/False

1. ___ Courage in a thing is when you no longer have misgivings about it.

2. ___ Courage is built as we exercise our God-given freedom to choose his will.

3. ___ We can be strong and courageous because we know God will always be with us.

4. ___ Courage cannot be exercised by taking "baby steps."

5. ___ Courage is something we take, not something we wait for.

KEY 11
REVIVE THROUGH REST

Quote of the Day

"In place of our exhaustion and spiritual fatigue, God will give us rest. All he asks is that we come to Him . . . that we spend a while thinking about Him, meditating on Him, talking to Him, listening in silence, occupying ourselves with Him—totally and thoroughly lost in the hiding place of His presence."

Charles Swindoll

Ever heard the phrase, "work hard, rest well"? There is a lot packed into those two little phrases. Some people may think that working long hours every day has more merit than resting well, but a good balance of both makes you a much more productive worker in the long run. Why? Because this is how we are designed—for work and rest. We are hard-wired for both. Yes, people try to get around the need for rest in many ways, but those efforts usually backfire at some point. Burnout is typically the result of ignoring the warning signs too long.

Rest is God's gift to keep us healthy and give us a full, happy life. Father knows that we find fulfillment when we work at something we enjoy doing, but he also knows that too much of a good thing is bad for us. In all our enthusiasm to finish our tasks, rest keeps us from hurting ourselves. We need regular breaks throughout the day. A full night sleep is essential for productivity as well as good health. Psalm 127:2 says, "In vain you rise early and stay up late, toiling for food to eat—for he grants sleep to those he loves."

Our brains especially prefer uninterrupted sleep and a consistent sleeping schedule. Young children need 11-12 hours per night, teenagers need 8-10 hours, and adults need 7-9 hours per night. Yes, this does not always work out in real life, but we can dream, can't we? Not only do we need regular breaks and regular sleep hours, but studies also show that we need one "hard break" (a Sabbath) every week when we are "unplugged." If you are not convinced that you need to regularly unplug, study the harmful effects of too much screen time, such as problems with self-worth, relational struggles, and the potential physical problems that go along with excessive screen use.

How rested do you usually feel? Is your body craving sleep? Are there some adjustments you could make to your working hours? Is anything preventing you from getting a good night sleep? Here's a challenge for you: If you need to start getting a better night's sleep, silence your devices one hour before bed, then don't take any of them to bed with you.

Restful habits you can try:

1. If possible, grab a nap whenever you can (not at work, of course.)
2. When you feel stressed or overly tired, take a moment to shut your eyes and breathe for at least a full minute.
3. Whenever you can, get a change of atmosphere. For example, if you work at home, go outside for a few moments, and find something beautiful to admire.
4. Put weekly rest breaks on your calendar and schedule other activities around those. These are times for you to do something you enjoy.

5. Plan yearly vacations, or at least a get-a-way. As soon as you complete one, plan your next one.

Keep in mind that get-a-ways don't need to be expensive. They can be as simple as taking a walk or just sitting beside a lake. Remember that new habits take 2-3 months to form, so don't give up too soon. Remember—work hard and rest well!

Meditate on it

Transforming the mind & emotions

Come to me, all who labor and are heavy laden, and I will give you rest. Take my yoke upon you, and learn from me, for I am gentle and lowly in heart, and you will find rest for your souls. For my yoke is easy, and my burden is light.

Matthew 11:28-30

1. Read it in context: Matthew 11:25-30
2. Say it out loud. Matthew 11:28-30
3. Write it down:

_____

_____

_____

_____

_____

_____

_____

_____

4. Pray it: (Example) "Lord, I need you! I've been working hard, and I'm worn out. I need your rest. Show me just what you would have me to do, no more, and no less. Thank you for understanding what I am going through and for being so gentle with me. I receive your rest right now. I'm laying down my heavy burdens and taking up the work that we will be doing together, which always seems light because we're yoked together."

5. Write down your prayer:

_____

_____

_____

_____

_____

_____

_____

_____

Discuss it
Share your thoughts

1. Describe your work-rest balance.
2. How could you get a better night's sleep?
3. What are some restful habits you would like to develop in your life?

Live it
Choose one or more activities, then write what happened.

1. Take regular breaks during the day.

2. Try to get your recommended amount of sleep each night (or each day if you work at night.)

3. Take one day off to unplug each week.

4. Enjoy a retreat

5. Let your soul soak in the presence of God for at least 15 minutes while you listen to God every day.

6. Get regular exercise. (Take a prayer walk.)

7. Read good books.

8. Take a nap wherever you can squeeze one in.

9. Play cards or a table game with friends.

10. Enjoy regular sit-down meals with family.

11. Sit down for a chat with a friend.

12. Be completely still and just breathe for a few minutes.

_____
_____
_____
_____
_____
_____
_____
_____

Quiz
True/False

1. ___ Long-term, when we refuse to rest, burnout is the inevitable result.

2. ___ Taking time to rest will prolong your life.

3. ___ We need one "hard break" every week for additional rest.

4. ___ Doing what God wants is a lot more stressful than doing what I want.

5. ___ One way to cultivate rest is by just being still and breathing for a few minutes.

KEY 12
EXPAND YOUR CREATIVITY

Quote of the Day

"As my sufferings mounted, I soon realized that there were two ways in which I could respond to my situation—either to react with bitterness or seek to transform the suffering into a creative force. I decided to follow the latter course."

Martin Luther King Jr.

Ever had a fantastic idea but could not make it happen? When you get ideas like that, don't discount them, or move on too fast. Take a moment and write down your thoughts. You never know what might happen. It could be that in the future you, (or someone you collaborate with), will discover how to make that idea work. That is part of what creativity is all about, patiently taking things in stages and being willing to go back and rework an idea several times until you get it right, asking for help in areas outside your expertise.

As a songwriter, I've learned through the years to compose in stages. I might get an initial chord progression, then add melody and lyrics later—or I may get the lyrics, then write the melody and find the supporting chords later. I've also experienced times when a song seems to be ready for publishing, but there is no market for it yet. While it can be discouraging to create something, no one is enjoying—but wait! God appreciates our creative attempts. He's like a smiling grandfather enjoying every moment we spend doing what we love to do in his presence. Every time we exercise our creative gifts, it is an act of worship to him.

God delights in every paragraph, stroke of the brush, stitch, note, or line of code. Why? Because when we create, we act like our Creator! God has made each of us in his image, and creativity is part of that image.

Maybe you think you're not very creative, but we are all creative in different ways. Your creative bent is uniquely yours. There will never be another person who is exactly like you or expresses themselves the way you do. The goal, then, is not to *become* creative but to seek to unlock the creative potential you *already* possess. Think of one thing you do reasonably well and enjoy doing. That is your baby! (Be careful about trying to be an expert in too many things at once.) Just start by picking one thing and staying with it until you are an expert. Practice it a thousand times until you own it. As you are doing it, tell God, "I'm doing this for you!"

Colossians 3:23 says, "Whatever you do, work heartily, as for the Lord . . . You are serving the Lord Christ." Be content with doing it for God, your audience of one—then there may come a day your gift will go public. Proverbs 22:29 says, "Do you see a man skillful in his work? He will stand before kings; he will not stand before obscure men."

Meditate on it
Transforming the mind & emotions

For we are his workmanship, created in Christ Jesus for good works, which God prepared beforehand, that we should walk in them.

Ephesians 2:10

1. Read it in context: Ephesians 2:1-10
2. Say it out loud. Ephesians 2:10

3. Write it down:

_____

_____

_____

_____

_____

_____

4. Pray it: "Father, thank you I am your workmanship, and you created me in Christ Jesus for all kinds of good works, including my creative endeavors. You already knew I would do these things and prepared me for them beforehand."

5. Write down your prayer:

_____

_____

_____

_____

_____

_____

_____

_____

_____

Discuss it
Share your thoughts

1. Share one creative idea you've had in the past that may hold some promise in the future.

2. Why does God like it when we express our creativity?

3. What is your creative bent? Talk about how you feel when you are doing that.

Live it

Choose one or more activities, then write what happened.

1. Explore new opportunities.

2. Take small steps of action in creative endeavors.

3. See each act of creativity as an act of worship.

4. Choose a skill you need to advance in and practice it to mastery.

5. Pray for creative insight.

6. Read the book, "Cure for the Common Life: Living in Your Sweet Spot" by Max Lucado

7. Discover ways to share with others the creative things you do.

8. Find a group that does what you do and do it together!

_____

_____

_____

_____

_____

_____

Quiz
True/False

1. ___ It's always a good idea to become an expert at as many things as you can.

2. ___ Practice your skill a thousand times until you really own it.

3. ___ God has always had full knowledge of all the good things you were created to do.

4. ___ Creative expression and worship are two completely different things.

5. ___ You can be divinely led as you explore new opportunities for creative expression.

KEY 13
LIVE IN FREEDOM

Quote of the Day

"So, if the Son sets you free, you will be free indeed."

John 8:36

When you say the word *freedom*, what comes to mind? If someone in Jesus' time were asked that question, they would have said, "freedom from the tyranny of Rome." The Jews were waiting for a Messiah who would free them from Roman occupation. As horrible as that was, the scope of Jesus' mission was vastly broader. Our heavenly Father sent Jesus to liberate not just the nation of Israel but all people from the tyranny of sin. Sin means "missing the mark"; it's about falling short. Romans 3:23 says, "For all have sinned and fall short of the glory of God." God has designed us to thrive on his glory. We are like trees that thrive on good soil, water, and sunshine, but we begin to wilt whenever we exchange God's glory for fake substitutes.

Father knows our propensity to walk into the enemy's traps, which is why he sent Jesus to free us. At the beginning of his public ministry, Jesus made this announcement: "The Spirit of the Lord is upon me because he has anointed me to proclaim good news to the poor. He has sent me to proclaim liberty to the captives and recovery of sight to the blind, to set at liberty those who are oppressed, to proclaim the year of the Lord's favor." (Luke 14:18-20) Our heavenly Father sent Jesus on a mission to bring us the best news we would ever hear—the good news that anyone willing to receive his gift of freedom would no longer be a victim of their past, no longer be blind to the truth, and no longer addicted.

Wow! How can that be? Here it is in a nutshell. For those who receive Christ, the death of Jesus paid the penalty for all our sin, and the resurrection of Christ Jesus enabled us to walk in his authority—to live in victory rather than victimization. Think of authority as a badge visible only in the spiritual realm respected by angels and demons alike. That is powerful! As citizens of the Kingdom of Heaven, we have the power to bind and to loose. Jesus said, "I will give you the keys of the kingdom of heaven, and whatever you bind on earth shall be bound in heaven, and whatever you loose on earth shall be loosed in heaven" (Matthew 16.19). This verse is saying that the keys he gives us operate in the earth realm as well as the realm of the spirit because, as Ephesians 2:5 says, we are "seated in heavenly places in Christ Jesus." Since we are in Christ, what we declare on the earth carries weight here on earth as well as in the spiritual realm.

Why then are so many Christians living in fear and victimization? Why are so many believers still in bondage to sinful habits? The answer is simple—because they continue to believe the devil's lies—thoughts that don't agree with God's Word, such as, "I am just a victim of my past." or "Everyone in my family line has the same problem; so, I'm stuck." I'd like to share with you a story from my own life that may bring you some hope, especially if there is an area of your life where you, or someone you know, could use some freedom.

My dad developed schizophrenia after the Korean War, and eventually left home when I was twelve years old, leaving my mother to care for her four children on her own. To make matters worse, I had severe scoliosis, night terrors and was suffering from extreme sensitivities to food, mold, pet dander, dust, pollen, and various chemicals. As things got progressively worse in my twenties, I decided to take some decisive steps of action. The first was to visit an allergy clinic to get tested. After a week of instruction and thorough testing, they sent me home with several different serums to give myself—which all stopped working about eight months later. Becoming more desperate, I decided to gather for prayer with some Godly young men from our church. After we got our hearts right before the Lord, they placed their hands on me and prayed. The Holy Spirit started doing his work. I felt as though every cell in my body was vibrating rapidly. At one point, I sensed waves going up and down my body from my feet to my head and back. A few minutes later, all the sensations subsided, and I sat up, feeling like a new man! I went home and began carefully testing various substances to monitor the extent of my healing. Every food sensitivity, as well as all the other sensitivities, were gone! I could eat all of the foods I was previously reacting to. I could breathe in the house without an air filter. I could visit the library or a clothing store because the formaldehyde sensitivity was gone. It was wonderful! (I was eventually freed from the night terrors as well. See "Key 17" for that story.)

We all have areas of our lives where we need to get free. These issues are not always related to demonic oppression, but they all require that we exercise our God-given authority. Don't wait for an emergency. Start investing in your freedom now! For a moment, think of your mind as an enclosed garden and God as your Master Gardener. He encourages you to plant good fruits, such as love, joy, peace, and self-control. Your garden also needs to be watched over. It can't be left untended; otherwise, weeds will begin to grow—things like hatred, bitterness, and laziness. Be on the lookout for incoming poison arrows. These are lies such as debilitating fear, doubt, unbelief, and despair. So, as you are working on planting good things and weeding out the bad—-defend your garden! Ephesians 6:10-12 says, "Finally, be strong in the Lord and in the strength of his might. Put on the whole armor of God that you may be able to stand against the schemes of the devil. For we do not wrestle against flesh and blood, but against the rulers, against the authorities, against the cosmic powers over this present darkness, against the spiritual forces of evil in the heavenly places."

Think of a bad habit you can't seem to change. It could be it does not change because there is a lie you continue to believe. Ask the Holy Spirit to help you identify your ungodly beliefs. If you don't know what thought pattern is behind your problem, that is ok—God does! Just get on your knees and humbly ask him to reveal to you the source of your trouble. He will be faithful to show you because it is not his will that you remain stuck. Once you discern the lie, disagree with it aloud, then begin to declare the truth from God's Word. For example, if you feel powerless in a situation, you could say, "I can do all things through Christ who strengthens me." As you continue to declare this truth, the truth will win out over the lie, and in God's perfect timing, you will be free! In John chapter 8, Jesus said, "If you hold to my teaching, you are really my disciples. Then you will know the truth, and the truth will set you free." How long does it take to get free? The answer to that is different for everyone. Some people get instantly free of at least some of their hang-ups when they receive Christ as Savior, and others (like me) seem to go through a longer process.

Is there an area of your life where you need deliverance or healing? Father wants to set you free! He wants to heal you. How and when that will happen is up to him, but he is waiting for *you* to take the initiative. Read the healing and deliverance stories of the New Testament. Notice who is usually the one taking action at the beginning of the story—the desperate one! Just know that God's will is for your complete freedom. Come to him and boldly ask for the liberty he wants to give you.

Meditate on it

Transforming the mind & emotions

Therefore, confess your sins to each other and pray for each other so that you may be healed.

James 5:16

1. Read it in context: James 5.15-16
2. Say it out loud. James 5:16
3. Write it down:

_____

_____

_____

_____

4. Pray it: "Lord, I confess to you my sin of _____. It has produced much grief for those close to me and great injury to myself as well. I know what I have done is wrong, and I renounce it now. I receive your forgiveness and healing now in Jesus' name. Amen!"

5. Write down your prayer:

_____

_____

_____

_____

_____

_____

_____

Discuss it
Share your thoughts

1. Discuss one aspect of freedom in Christ that is exciting to you.

2. What is one way the enemy tries to entrap people?

3. Why do so many Christians stay living in victimization?

4. Name one area in your life where you need to gain freedom. What lie have you been believing? What truth from God's Word will you begin declaring this week?

Live it

Choose one or more activities, then write what happened

1. Confess any known personal sin and put it under the Blood of Christ.
2. Break generational bondagers by confessing the sin of your ancestors as God reveals.
3. Forgive others who have offended you.
4. Renounce any association with the occult, then destroy and remove any occult artifacts in your home.
5. Regularly meditate on God's Word. (James 1:25) "the perfect law of freedom"
6. Put off old bad habits and develop good new ones (Ephesians 4:22-32).
7. Give yourself to daily worship and prayer.

_____

_____

_____

_____

_____

_____

_____

_____

_____

_____

_____

_____

_____

Quiz
True/False

1. ___ To be free means I can do whatever I want!

2. ___ Freedom from bondage to an addiction always requires a lengthy recovery period.

3. ___ Often, desperation is what best prepares someone to be free from a sinful habit.

4. ___ When it comes to sinful habits and healing, deal with it privately.

5. ___ Breaking generational bondage is a powerful way to gain new freedom in your life.

KEY 14
WORSHIP IN EVERYTHING

Quote of the Day

"We are perishing for lack of wonder, not for lack of wonders."
GK Chesterton

When we catch even a glimpse of the majesty and love of God, we are filled with amazement—just like the angels in heaven when they see another side of God's glory. The book of Revelation paints a picture for us of what worship is like in heaven: In Revelation chapter 4, it says, "The twenty-four elders and the four living creatures fell down and worshiped God, who was seated on the throne. And they cried: "Amen, Hallelujah!" Then a voice came from the throne, saying: "Praise our God, all you his Servants, You who fear him, both great and small!" Then I heard what sounded like a great multitude, like the roar of rushing waters and like loud peals of thunder, shouting: "Hallelujah! For our, Lord God Almighty reigns. Let us rejoice and be glad and give him glory! For the wedding of the Lamb has come, and his bride has made herself ready."

Here is what we find in that passage: worship leaders, a call to worship, falling prostrate, thunderous shouting, and rejoicing over the bride (which is yet another picture of who we are in Christ.) But here on earth, the reality for most of us is that we're not always in awe of God, and sometimes we don't even feel like worshiping, let alone falling down. We need a little help—and God knows that.

That's why he's the one who initiates. John 6:44 says, "No one can come to me unless the Father who sent me draws him." Worship is like a dance. He leads, and we respond. As it says in I John, "God is love" (I John 4:8). He loves us because that's the essence of who he is—and verse 19 says, "We love because he first loved us." He leads. We respond. What Jesus has done for us is so amazing! Our Creator has become our Father. Jesus is God in bodily form, the one who laid down his life for us and now lives within us by his Spirit. Not only that, but (whether we are aware of it or not), he keeps loving us every moment of our lives.

The secret of entering into deeper worship is becoming more aware of God, watching for him, discerning his heart, and discovering what he is doing. Yes, sometimes it seems like a battle to get there; but remember, as long as we are on the earth, our enemy, the devil, will be working hard on doing all he can to prevent us from worshiping God.

When Jesus began his public ministry, Satan tempted him to take a shortcut to the finish line. Here's what it says in Matthew, chapter 4: "Again, the devil took him to a very high mountain and showed him all the kingdoms of the world and their splendor. "All this I will give you," he said, "if you will bow down and worship me" (Matthew 4:8-9). Jesus' response was, "Away from me, Satan! For it is written: 'Worship the Lord your God and serve him only'" (Matthew 4:10).

As God's sons and daughters, we are faced with the same temptation—the pull to set our desires on something other than God, which the Bible calls idolatry. When the devil tempts you to place all of your affections on something other than God, give him the same reply Jesus did, "Away from me, Satan. It is written: Worship the Lord your God and serve him only." What is written in God's Word is the sword that we wield against the enemy. The first commandment is: "You shall have no other gods before me." Take a moment to let the Holy Spirit search your heart. Who is number one in your affections right now?

There two basic modes of worship: the way we live unto God and the way we express ourselves to God. Here's an illustration: A good poem has both "words and music." The poem's words are the text, and its music is the beauty of the meter, accent, and rhyme. Your life is a worship poem. The words of your poem are the way you live unto God, and the music of your poem is the way you express yourself to God.

Let's take a look at the content of your life poem first. Worship is whatever you do as unto the Lord (Colossians 3:23). The one who faithfully does the laundry or washes the dishes for the glory of God is worshiping God. Father loves every intentional, heart-felt act that we do to honor him. So, the next time you go to work, intentionally do it for the Lord.

Then there's your expression of worship—the meter and the rhyme of your love for God. It's the singing, dancing, shouting, and lifting of your hands. These are all wonderful ways to worship, provided they are motivated by love for God. By the way, you don't have to have a good singing voice to worship. Scripture says, "Man looks on the outward appearance, but the Lord looks on the heart." If your heart is singing along with your voice, that's what matters most!

Worship comes with plenty of benefits. The greatest of all rewards is that God receives the glory. But worship also helps us. God encourages us to worship because it's the only thing that genuinely quenches our soul's thirst. It's the atmosphere of heaven that we breathe. Worship is the richest of foods that satisfy our appetite for intimacy. In an atmosphere of worship, our souls are cleansed and healed. That's important—because there's a lot of "road dirt" out there that tends to build up in our souls. We need to have our hearts washed regularly.

Finally, we benefit when we worship God because we become like whatever we worship. So, the more we worship God, the more we become like him. As the Bride of Christ, we become transformed as we gaze upon him. Song of Solomon is a book of the Bible that is all about intimacy. It's a poetic account of passionate love between a lover and the beloved. It's in God's Word because intimacy is in the heart of God. It's our primary reason for being. He made us for love, but sometimes other things get in the way, and we lose sight of the truth. Jesus is the truth. He's the one who deserves all our adoration.

Meditate on it

Transforming the mind & emotions

I appeal to you, therefore, brothers, by the mercies of God, to present your bodies as a living sacrifice, holy and acceptable to God, which is your spiritual worship.

Romans 12:1

1. Read it in context: Romans 12:1-8
2. Say it out loud. Romans 12:1
3. Write it out:

_____

_____

_____

_____

_____

_____

_____

_____

4. Pray it: "Father, thank you for your mercy. I am yours. In view of all you have done for me, I take my everyday life and place it before you as an offering of worship—my sleeping, eating, work-life, relationships, recreation, giving, praying, praising, and my function in the local church."
5. Write down your prayer.

_____

_____

_____

_____

_____

Discuss it
Share your thoughts

1. What is God currently doing in your life?
2. How are you being tempted to place your affections on something other than God? What steps will you take to overcome this temptation?
3. Discuss what it looks like to worship God with your life.
4. What can you do to increase your expression of worship to God?

Live it
Choose one or more activities, then write what happened

1. Talk to God and listen to him throughout the day.
2. Express gratefulness. Make music to the Lord!
3. Serve others with a good attitude.
4. Listen carefully to the wisdom of Godly teachers and apply what you learn.
5. Give your whole heart in worship to God with other believers.
6. Exercise God-honoring creativity.
7. Humbly confess your sin.
8. Diligently study and meditate on the Word.
9. Daily care for your physical body.
10. Joyfully steward your home and resources.
11. Take moments to enjoy God's creation.
12. Exercise your spiritual gifts. (See Key 16)

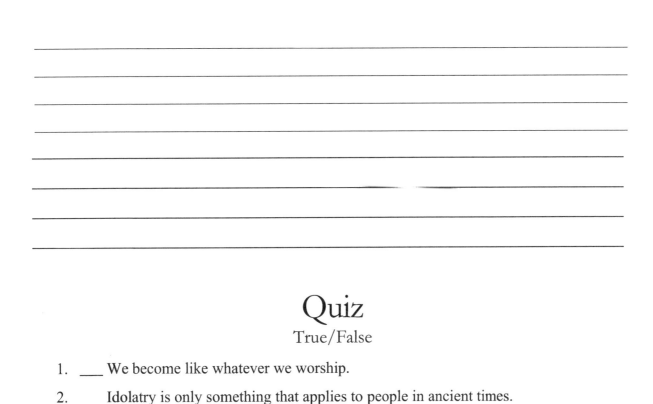

Quiz
True/False

1. ___ We become like whatever we worship.

2. ___ Idolatry is only something that applies to people in ancient times.

3. ___ The way you carry out the activities of the day has nothing to do with worship.

4. ___ Entering into worship from the heart cleanses the soul.

5. ___ We become like whatever we worship.

KEY 15
GROW IN GENEROSITY

Quote of the Day

"We make a living by what we get, but we make life by what we give."
Winston Churchill

God's nature is to be generous. As image-bearers, each of us has the potential for generosity, regardless of how wealthy we think we are. Some people give liberally and instantly, without counting the cost. It seems that the more they give, the more joyful they become.

Were they just born that way? No, they discovered the gift of generosity and the joy that goes with it. That's the main benefit of giving—you identify with how God feels when he gives. It is habit-forming. The more you give, the more joy you get, leading to more sharing and even more enjoyment. Acts 20:35 says, "It is more blessed to give than to receive."

Besides an increase in joy, another benefit of the gift of generosity is—you receive a return on your investment. There's an ancient law called the law of sowing and reaping. It works like gravity, whether you are aware of it or not. Paul talks about this law in Galatians 6:7, "Whatever a man sows, this he will also reap." Of course, this is not referring just to money; it's about everything! If I show kindness to someone, I will reap kindness. If I keep reacting in anger, others will be angry with me as well. This law governs the giving of material things too. Jesus said, "And if anyone gives even a cup of cold water to one of these little ones who is my disciple, truly I tell you, that person will certainly not lose their reward." God notices and remembers those (so called) "little efforts" you make to bless others — and will reward you. (II Corinthians 5:10).

You'll also be happy to know that the return you get on giving to people is always more than the gift's size. Luke 6:38 says, "Give, and it will be given to you. A good measure, pressed down, shaken together, and running over, will be poured into your lap." When we give, God notices the measure we use, then gives us a greater return. It's "pressed down, shaken together, and running over." You can't out-give God!

Having said that, we need to remember that the law of sowing and reaping does not stand alone. It is a fundamental principle, but only one layer of the truth. The law must be coupled together with other guiding principles from God's Word.

There are four commands from Scripture that surround and give context to the law of sowing and reaping:

Principle #1: Give regularly and generously—not just because there is a need to give to, but because it's God's nature to give. Hoarding is a form of idolatry—which means setting our affections on something other than God. So, keep giving unselfishly as the Spirit leads.

Principle #2: Check your heart's motivation. Give because you genuinely care about people, not for any selfish reason.

Jesus said, "Thus when you give to the needy, sound no trumpet before you, as the hypocrites do in the synagogues and in the streets that they may be praised by others. Truly, I say to you, they have received their reward. But when you give to the needy, do not let your left hand know what your right hand is doing so that your giving may be in secret. And your Father who sees in secret will reward you." **(Matthew 6:2-4)** In other words, when you give— don't muse over what you are doing; just do it.

Principle #3: Be content with what you have. The tenth commandment is, "Thou shalt not covet." Coveting means taking delight in something in the wrong way. I Timothy 6:10 says, "The love of money is the root of all evil." Notice that it's not money itself that is evil, but the love of money. There is nothing wrong with having money and possessions, but there is a big problem when those things have you!

Principle #4: Invest in eternal things. Matthew 6:19-21 says, "Do not lay up for yourselves treasures on earth, where moth and rust destroy and where thieves break in and steal, but lay up for yourselves treasures in heaven, where neither moth nor rust destroys and where thieves do not break in and steal. For where your treasure is, there your heart will be also." Life is short compared to all eternity, so focus on eternal investments, such as unselfish giving, encouragement, and acts of kindness.

Here's a story from my own life that illustrates this teaching, showing what can happen when we give, even in the simplest of ways. For many years I taught in private Christian schools. My wife and I learned to live and be content with what we had. This kind of lifestyle left the door open for God to do all sorts of financial miracles for us, some great and some small.

One day Meg called me in my classroom to remind me that a friend of ours was having a birthday and needed to make out a card. We usually tried to put at least some cash in each card, but I only had $4 left in my wallet this particular day. So, I put $4 inside the card. Later that same day, we were given a check for $400 from someone that told us God had asked them to write one to us for that specific amount!

So, every day, listen to God about what you could give, whether it's a word of encouragement, some flowers, a meal, or even some cash. Tithe regularly to your local church. (That means to give 10% of your income.) Also, look for opportunities to give offerings—anything beyond your tithe. Finally, exercise generous giving in the context of the four principles from Scripture mentioned above: regular giving, proper motivation, contentment, and eternal investment.

Meditate on it

Transforming the mind & emotions

Whoever sows sparingly will also reap sparingly, and whoever sows bountifully will also reap bountifully. Each one must give as he has decided in his heart, not reluctantly or under compulsion, for God loves a cheerful giver.

II Corinthians 9:6-7

1. Read it in context: II Corinthians 9:1-15
2. Say it out loud. II Corinthians 9:6-7
3. Write it down:

_____

_____

_____

_____

_____

_____

4. Pray it: "Father, thank you for all you have given me. Enlarge my heart that I would be a more cheerful giver, not just of my income, but of my time and love as well."

5. Write down your prayer:

_____

_____

_____

_____

_____

Discuss it
Share your thoughts

1. In what ways could you become more generous?
2. What is the main reason that you give to others?
3. In what ways could you become more content?

Live it
Choose one or more activities, then write what happened

1. Make a list of things you are grateful for.
2. Pay your tithe immediately after you receive a paycheck.
3. Pick a charity and give to it regularly.
4. Fund a cause based on your passions.
5. Find someone to support who is working on a worthy cause.
6. Spend time with generous people.
7. Trim down your expenses where possible.
8. Sell items you no longer need and give at least a portion to the needy.
9. Set up a "master has need" cash account and be ready to give as needs arise.

_____

_____

_____

_____

_____

_____

_____

_____

_____

Quiz

True/False

1. ___ We should focus on eternal investments.

2. ___ You should give because you know you will get something for yourself.

3. ___ Money is the root of all evil.

4. ___ God rewards generous, heartfelt giving.

5. ___ Thankful people tend to be very generous.

KEY 16
EXERCISE YOUR SPIRITUAL GIFTS

Quote of the Day

"Wherever the Holy Ghost has right of way, the gifts of the Spirit will be in manifestation; and where these gifts are never in manifestation, I question whether he is present."

Smith Wigglesworth

Jesus came to earth to prove and multiply his love. He gave his disciples authority to do the things they saw him doing–to heal the sick, cast out demons, and raise the dead. Jesus said we would do *"greater* works" (John 14:12), which means his mission was only the beginning. He came to partner with us in his work, multiplying his love to millions, but he knew we could not do it alone. Jesus said he would not leave us as orphans (John 14:18) and promised to send the Holy Spirit, aka "The Helper" or "The Advocate" (John 16:7-11). He wants to reveal his wisdom, inspire others through us, and work miracles through us, but it only happens when we yield to his Holy Spirit living within us. Of course, we don't all have the same gifts. I Corinthians 12:7 says, "To each is given the manifestation of the Spirit for the common good." God loves harmony! (Psalm 133; John 17) Just as each choir member sings their assigned line, each member of the church exercises functions in their assigned roles.

Ministry Gifts (Ephesians 4.11-13)

1. Apostles
2. Prophets
3. Evangelists
4. Pastors
5. Teachers

Manifestation Gifts (I Corinthians 12)

1. The Word of Wisdom: divine wisdom or the right application of knowledge.
2. The Word of Knowledge: facts God has revealed to us to encourage others in a particular situation
3. The Discerning of Spirits: the believer is enabled to know what is motivating a person or situation immediately
4. The Gift of Prophecy: telling something that God has spontaneously brought to mind
5. Different Kinds of Tongues: languages that are not naturally acquired for worship, praise, or prayer (Jude 1.20), edifying the church, or as a sign to unbelievers (I Cor. 14)
6. Interpretation of Tongues: the translation of languages that have not been naturally acquired
7. The Gift of Faith: a sudden surge of faith, usually in a crisis, to confidently believe without a doubt
8. Gifts of Healing: removing diseases from the spirit, soul, or body
9. Working of Miracles: a supernatural ability to serve others as a channel of God's miracle-working power

Motivational Gifts (Romans 12:6-8)

1. Prophesying
2. Serving
3. Teaching
4. Encouraging
5. Giving
6. Leading
7. Showing Mercy

Recommended Reading:

- *Understanding Spiritual Gifts* by Kay Arthur
- *Discover Your God-Given Gifts* by Don and Katie Fortune
- *Spiritual Gifts: What They Are and Why They Matter by Thomas R. Schreiner*
- *S.H.A.P.E.: Finding and Fulfilling Your Unique Purpose for Life* by Erik Rees

Meditate on it
Transforming the mind & emotions

All these are empowered by one and the same Spirit, who apportions to each one individually as he wills.

I Corinthians 12:11

1. Read it in context: I Corinthians 12:4-11
2. Say it out loud. I Corinthians 12:11
3. Write it out:

_____

_____

_____

_____

_____

_____

_____

_____

_____

4. Pray it: (Example) "Jesus, thank you for sending the Holy Spirit, our helper, and our advocate with the Father. I want to be used by you, so equip me with the spiritual gifts you have in mind for me."
5. Write down your prayer:

_____

_____

_____

_____

_____

_____

_____

_____

Discuss it
Share your thoughts

1. Which gift (or gifts) of the Holy Spirit do you see operating in your life? Tell about it.

2. Which gift of the Holy Spirit would you like to begin operating in? What would that look like?

3. What are the fillings of the Holy Spirit? Why are they important?

Live it
Choose one or more activities, then write what happened

1. Pursue love first and foremost. All the gifts operate out of love and no other motivation. (Remember, regardless of what your life is like—you are loved!)

2. Ask the Holy Spirit for a fresh filling every day

3. Ask those who know you well to share what they believe your spiritual gifts are.

4. Write down what the Holy Spirit is saying to you and doing through you. (This will help confirm what you discover through the assessments.)

_____

_____

_____

_____

_____

_____

_____

_____

_____

_____

_____

_____

_____

Quiz
True/False

1. ___ Jesus came to earth only to save us from our sins.

2. ___ We can't do God's work in God's way without the Holy Spirit's power.

3. ___ Each believer must operate in all nine gifts of the Holy Spirit.

4. ___ The filling of the Holy Spirit only happens once in your life.

5. ___ The gifts of the Spirit are primary. Love is in the background.

KEY 17
PRACTICE PERSEVERANCE

Quote of the Day

" God knows our situation; He will not judge us as if we had no difficulties to overcome. What matters is the sincerity and perseverance of our will to overcome them."

CS Lewis

We have all made mistakes and have suffered for them, and most of us also have, at one point or other, been victimized by wrongs committed by others. But regardless, it is comforting to know that God will still enable us to fulfill his purpose for our lives. God's "GPS" works on our behalf to get us rerouted regardless of who did what to whom.

Proverbs 16:9 says, "The heart of man plans his way, but the Lord establishes his steps." Rest assured; the Lord orchestrates all your steps. If you feel like you got off track somehow, don't worry! God's got you! He's already arranged another route to get you where you need to be.

Here are some examples from Scripture of God orchestrating the lives of his people despite their failure and victimization:

- Abraham (Genesis 12-25) means "Father of many nations," but he and his wife were too old to have children. Initially, Abraham tried to orchestrate the promise in his strength; but in the end, the promise came true in God's way.

- Jacob (Genesis 25-50) was the father of the 12 tribes of Israel. He started as a trickster, stealing his brother's birthright—which resulted in fleeing to another land for many years. To make matters worse, Jacob received a taste of his own medicine at the hand of his Father-in-law, Laban. Nevertheless, as he continued to persevere, Jacob received all God had promised.

- Job was the first book of the Bible to be written. (The "law of first mention" tells us that this book is key to interpreting other verses in the Bible on the topic of suffering.) In a nutshell—this story is about persevering through intense trials and persecution, then finishing well.

- Peter was the most reckless of the twelve disciples of Jesus. He would say something extraordinary one moment, then totally miss the mark the next. Peter's greatest failure was denying Jesus. In the end, Jesus restored him, and he became one of the greatest of the apostles.

Each one of those heroes of the faith mentioned had one thing in common– *they did not give up*, even when they had personally failed miserably or had been the victim of something outside their control (as in the case of Job and Jacob.) God wants to encourage us to push through in life despite the roadblocks. It is no wonder there are over one hundred verses in the Bible about perseverance. Here are some phrases used in those scriptures: "remain steadfast under trial," "do not grow weary of doing good," "run with endurance the race," "let steadfastness have its full effect," "do not grow weary in doing good," "if we endure, we will also reign with him," and "endurance produces character." For a great book on this subject, read Failing Forward: Turning Mistakes into Stepping Stones for Success by John C Maxwell.

I'd like to conclude by sharing my own story of perseverance. In Key 13," I talked about how I was delivered and healed from severe sensitivities to food and many other substances. Today I'd like to tell you the story of my fight with night terrors. I can remember how, as a young boy, I would wake up screaming in the night. My mother would come into my room to check on me, then I would go back to sleep, and it would happen all over again.

As the years went by, it seemed to get worse. During my five years of living on a university campus, each of my roommates would hear me yelling in the night and see me sleep-walking in the room. But the real test came after marriage. I would often lift my wife out of bed during the night to "protect her" from something I saw in a dream. We were both injured repeatedly during these episodes. I spent many nights sleeping on the couch and even tried tying my wrists to the headboard of our bed! All of this put a high amount of stress on our marriage.

At one point, I went to a sleep clinic where they wired me up and watched with horror all that happened during the night. They prescribed medication, but it only made things worse! It was then we knew it was going to take a miracle. Of course, many people prayed for me—friends, church leaders, and guest speakers—but there would be tremendous backlash from the demonic realm each time we prayed.

Finally, in my mid-fifties, after over 50 years of suffering, and seeking God, Meg and I heard about a healing room in our city that was staffed by trained Christian volunteers. These were people who regularly operated in the gifts of the Spirit and were accustomed to seeing God bring healing and deliverance to people. I was halfway expecting our prayer time with them would be long, and we would encounter tremendous resistance from the enemy, as in the past. But these people had already been praying and asking God for direction before we even entered the room. So, moments after we were in prayer together, a mild, soft-spoken man (who did not seem very eloquent) asked this question, "Have any of your family ever been involved in Free Masonry? I quickly answered, "Yes. My uncle was heavily into Free Masonry while he was alive." (I'm thinking now my uncle may not have realized that the oaths he took as part of that secret society were perpetuating spiritual bondage. He probably did not know his words would negatively impact our family.) The team we were praying with showed me what to pray to break that bondage. After I had renounced the source of the problem and placed it under the blood of Jesus, the night terrors stopped that very night! For a brief time, there were flickers of resistance, but I held my ground. To this day, I can sleep in bed all night. I feel more rested now in my 60's than I ever have in my whole life! I used to fall asleep during school staff meetings and at red lights, but now I feel like a new man!

Are you experiencing a significant struggle in an area of your life? Does it seem like things just never get better? You're not alone! Just remember, those who persevere through their trials and continue to seek God for solutions are victorious in the end. Remember James 1.12, "Blessed is the one who perseveres under trial because, having stood the test, that person will receive the crown of life that the Lord has promised to those who love him." (NIV)

Meditate on it
Transforming the mind & emotions

Therefore, since we are surrounded by so great a cloud of witnesses, let us also lay aside every weight and sin which clings so closely, and let us run with endurance the race that is set before us, looking to Jesus, the founder and perfecter of our faith, who for the joy that was set before him endured the cross, despising the shame, and is seated at the right hand of the throne of God.

Hebrews 12:1-2

1. Read it in context: Hebrews 11-12
2. Say it out loud. Hebrews 12:1-2
3. Write it out:

_____

_____

_____

_____

_____

_____

_____

_____

_____

4. Pray it: Lord, thank you for the example of those who persevered and finished their race. I choose **today** to lay aside those things that are weighing me down as I run. I look to you, Jesus, the founder, and perfecter of my faith. You endured the cross and all the shame. You are seated as the victor, and you have made me a victor too!

5. Write **down** your prayer:

_____
_____
_____
_____
_____
_____
_____
_____
_____

Discuss it
Share your thoughts

1. What roadblocks are you sensing in your life right now? (i.e., your past failures, mistreatment by others, etc.)
2. In what area are you tempted to give up?
3. What is one thing God would have you pursue at this time in your life?

Live it
Choose one or more activities, then write what happened

1. Separate yourself from your failure. You may fail at something—but *you* are not a failure! Say that out loud: "I am not a failure!" I am a victor in Christ!
2. Discern whether you actually failed at something—or whether the expectations were unrealistic to begin with.

3. Learn from things that happen without reacting to what happens. The next time you fail at something, ask yourself, "What can I learn from this?"

4. Learn to live with your defeats, and always stay grateful. The next time you feel defeated, say something you are thankful for.

5. Ask the Holy Spirit to help you see your "failures" from a different perspective.

6. Gain new insights from your experiences and take action on what you have learned.

7. Find mentors who can help you overcome areas where you are weak.

8. Refuse to meditate on past failures.

9. Change yourself, rather than expecting that others will change.

10. Get over yourself and start to give of yourself.

_____

_____

_____

_____

_____

_____

Quiz
True/False

1. ____ God is comfortable with our faltering.

2. ____ Once you make a mistake, it changes the outcome of your entire life.

3. ____ Successful people have this in common—they don't give up when there are mistakes or setbacks.

4. ____ We'll still succeed as long as we just keep ignoring areas of sin in our lives.

5. ____ If we persevere through trials, we will receive the crown of life.

KEY 18
FILL UP WITH GRATITUDE

Quote of the Day

"The one thing that cannot be taken away from a man is his ability to choose how he reacts to any given situation."

Victor Frankl

Gratitude is one of the most dynamic attitudes a human being can have. It's a quality that comes with great rewards but requires daily exercise. I Thessalonians 5:18 says, "Give thanks in all circumstances; for this is the will of God in Christ Jesus for you." Notice the verse does not call for us to give thanks *for* all circumstances. It says to be thankful *in* all circumstances. Though we cannot change the hand dealt to us, we can still make choices that will lead to winning the game in the end. Consistently grateful people are winners! They are the happiest people on earth!

According to recent studies, here are some of the benefits for people who regularly practice gratefulness.

They tend to:

- make new friends more easily.
- have overall better personal health.
- maintain better mental health.
- sleep better at night.
- have better self-esteem.

- enjoy better marriages.

What should be your focus right now—the positive thoughts you have about your future or the negative ones? Remember, the more you focus and verbalize your hope for a bright future, the brighter your future will eventually become. As someone has said, "Don't put a question mark where God puts a period." Some days, it seems easier to question or complain than be to be grateful; but is it worth it in the end?

According to a recent study, chronic complaining (where the complaint has no real purpose) has several very adverse effects:

1. Every time you entertain a negative thought, it is much easier to have another. In other words, negativity is highly addictive.
2. Complaining hurts relationships.
3. The stress produced from negativity releases elevated levels of cortisol, a stress hormone. Stress raises blood pressure and increases the risk of heart disease.
4. Research from Stanford University has shown that complaining shrinks the hippocampus— an area of the brain critical to problem-solving and intelligent thought. By the way—the hippocampus is one of the primary brain areas destroyed by Alzheimer's disease.

God is a good Father. He only wants the best for his children, which is why Scripture is full of admonition to be thankful. God urges us to be grateful for our protection and happiness. Yes, there will always be times when we need to work through a negative situation, but there's usually a positive way to handle it. In the end, we get better results in life when we are grateful.

We can all be thankful for something. When you first wake up in the morning, before your feet hit the ground, say at least one thing for which you are grateful. Who is the first person you usually see in the morning? Say something to them that you're glad about. They may or may not reciprocate, but that does not matter. You are not responsible for their response, only your own. Besides, what have you got to lose? It will undoubtedly have a better effect than complaining!

Keep in mind that attitudes create atmospheres. Gratitude usually inspires positivity. Most people tend to be more grateful when they are in an atmosphere of appreciation; so, make the atmosphere, and someone else will join in with you. Remember "Pigpen" in the peanuts cartoon? He carried a cloud of dust around him wherever he went. Well, you can create a cloud of gratitude that goes wherever you go. Try it. It's contagious!

As you go through a typical day, negative things will occur. You may need to do some problem-solving, so go for it—but as you do, maintain that atmosphere of gratitude. As you work, under your breath, rehearse what you are most grateful for. You'll find that as you make this a habit, your life will take on a more positive glow, and people will enjoy associating with you—which may lead to even better job performance.

Consider starting a gratitude log. List the good things you can see, family, friends, work, the income you do have, church, etc. Then list what you perceive in the unseen realm: your relationship with God, his love for you, his joy, his peace, his protection, and your future home in heaven. Exercise the gift of gratitude by reading the Psalms aloud. As you do this, your spirit will gain strength. Find a Psalm that's full of thanksgiving. Read it through, then on the second time, pray it from your heart out loud in your own words. As you continue this practice every day, note the good things that start happening in your life.

Here's another idea: Take just one verse and say it repeatedly aloud to the Lord throughout the day, especially if you are going through a stressful time of life. Here are some declarations you can make out loud amid any painful experience you might be going through:

1. Thank you, God, that you are in complete control (Isaiah 46:9-10).

2. Thank you, God, that your love and mercies never cease (Lamentations 3:22-23).

3. Thank you, Jesus, that you will never leave or forsake me (Hebrews 13:5).

4. Thank you, Holy Spirit, that you are with me in my affliction (Isaiah 43:2).

5. Thank you, Father, that you hear my every prayer (Psalms 34:17).

6. Thank you, Father, that you use my affliction to make me more like Christ (Romans 8:28–29).

7. Thank you Jesus that you have saved me, washed away my sins, and adopted me (Romans 4:7).

Meditate on it

Transforming the mind & emotions

Finally, brothers, whatever is true, whatever is honorable, whatever is just, whatever is pure, whatever is lovely, whatever is commendable, if there is any excellence, if there is anything worthy of praise, think about these things.

Philippians 4:8

1. Read it in context: Philippians 4:4-8
2. Say it out loud. Philippians 4:8

3. Write it out:

_____

_____

_____

_____

_____

_____

_____

4. Pray it: Father, I'm choosing today to think about the good things rather than the bad. Show me what is true, honorable, just, pure, lovely, commendable, excellent, and worthy of praise. Those will be the things I will focus on today.

5. Write down your prayer.

_____

_____

_____

_____

_____

_____

_____

Discuss it
Share your thoughts

1. What does it look like to be thankful <u>in</u> all circumstances?

2. Share how being more grateful would help you.

3. What are some hopeful thoughts you have about your future right now?

4. What is one way that you can be more grateful every day?

Live it

Choose one or more activities, then write what happened

1. Write in your journal the things you are thankful for.

2. Tell stories of good things that have happened in your life and family.

3. Find ways to serve the needy.

4. Show your appreciation by making gifts for people.

5. Sing songs that are full of positive themes.

6. Tell God what you are thankful for.

7. Look at pictures of people and events for whom you are grateful.

8. Shut down negativity. Don't allow yourself to complain habitually.

9. Apologize for being negative.

10. Forgive anyone who has hurt you, even if they did not ask for forgiveness. (Remember— forgiving others frees *you*!)

_____

_____

_____

_____

_____

_____

_____

_____

_____

Quiz
True/False

1. ___ Sometimes, you cannot choose how you will react to a given situation.

2. ___ The health of your body has nothing to do with the words you speak.

3. ___ Negativity can be addictive.

4. ___ We injure ourselves mentally and physically by continually focusing on things that are not true, dishonorable, unjust, and impure.

5. ___ Serving the needy is a great way to cultivate gratefulness.

KEY 19
BE RICHLY CONTENT

Quote of the Day

"Contentment makes a poor person rich, and discontent makes a rich person poor."
Benjamin Franklin

Who are the happiest people on earth? Those who are content with what they have! God always knows better than we do what will truly make us happy. Of all the ten commandments, the 10th one, "You shall not covet," seems to be the one most difficult to follow. Why is that? One reason is that it is the only commandment strictly about our thought life. The other is that it's a sin that is so easy to commit.

When we covet, it's another way of saying to God— "You have not provided for me very well. I would prefer to have what someone else has!" Not only that, but covetous thoughts can also make things awkward between you and another person. Part of genuine love for others is to rejoice with them when they succeed—but that is impossible if you are nursing a covetous thought.

Coveting is different for each one of us. Some of us desire other people's money, some focus on people's possessions, and others may fantasize about having a relationship that does not belong to us. Whatever gets you "peeking over the fence" in your thoughts, desiring what someone else has—that is your "little dragon." So, repent quickly before the little dragon grows up and becomes a full-grown beast! Slay the dragon of covetousness now before it consumes you!

You might be saying, "Hey, everybody does that! It's no sin to want something." And you would be right. It's no sin to want something, but it is wrong to desire something in the possession of someone else! The 10th commandment says: "You shall not covet anything that is your neighbor's."

Pretend God granted you three wishes, letting you have things belonging to someone else. Would you be happy if your wishes were all granted? Probably not. You would discover that having these things created a whole new batch of problems to solve! Remember when you were a child, wanting something someone else had? For many of us, it's not too different now, except that the toys now cost more, and the consequences for translating covetous thoughts into action are graver.

King David loved God with all his heart, but he found out the hard way just how expensive it is to covet. He desired another man's wife, so much he ordered to have her brought to him so that he could have sex with her. Then he arranged to have her husband killed so that he could have her as his wife. As a result, David experienced some painful consequences. (Read about it II Samuel through I Kings, chapter 2.) That is what it can look like when the little dragon of "covetousness" is treated as a pet. It eventually grows up and wreaks havoc in your life!

God has a better way for us. Because of his great love for us, he wants to protect us from our own heart's propensities. Yes, the world is continually chanting, "follow your heart," "listen to your heart," "If it feels good, do it." But the world doesn't understand the heart. God's Word tells us that humanity is *not* naturally good. Jeremiah 17:9 says, "The heart is deceitful above all things, and desperately sick; who can understand it? And Romans 3:23 says, "For all have sinned and fall short of the glory of God." We cannot depend upon our unregenerate hearts for guidance. King David listened to his covetous heart and look where it got him! We can't always depend upon our hearts for advice, but here are some steps we can take to start winning in this area:

1. Depend upon the Holy Spirit. Ask him to reveal any covetousness in you.

2. By the authority you have in Christ, put that sin under the blood. Jesus paid for it all on the cross, which gives you free access to heaven, but to live free here on earth, you need a clear conscience. So go to God in prayer and put that specific sin under the blood of Jesus.

3. Thank God for your relationships, for what God has provided you with, and for your great inheritance in Christ.

Keep doing this every day. As you go through life, continue to slay those little dragons while they are still young, and contentment should become your new normal. (Read I Timothy 6:6-9).

Meditate on it
Transforming the mind & emotions

Finally, brothers, whatever is true, whatever is honorable, whatever is just, whatever is pure, whatever is lovely, whatever is commendable, if there is any excellence, if there is anything worthy of praise, think about these things.

Philippians 4:8

1. Read it in context: Philippians 4:8-9
2. Say it out loud: Philippians 4:8

3. Write it out:

_____

_____

_____

_____

_____

_____

_____

_____

4. Pray it: "Lord, today I choose to think on the things that are true, honorable, just, pure, lovely, commendable, and excellent. May they drown out anything that is otherwise."

5. Write down your prayer.

_____

_____

_____

_____

_____

_____

_____

_____

_____

Discuss it
Share your thoughts

1. What do you tend to covet the most? Why?

2. How does covetousness wreak havoc in your life?

3. How can you become more content?

Live it

Choose one or more activities, then write what happened

1. Ask forgiveness for negative thinking and speaking

2. Seek first the Kingdom of God (Matthew 6:33)

3. Live a life of worship.

4. Retell stories of the good things God has done

5. Thank God and others out loud every day.

6. Learn to trust God for daily provision.

7. Be careful not to gaze at things you are not allowed to possess

_____

_____

_____

_____

_____

_____

_____

_____

Quiz
True/False

1. ___ The happiest people on earth are those who have everything they want.

2. ___ Coveting is desiring something in possession of somebody else.

3. ___ I'll know when I need to stop coveting when a friend tells me to stop.

4. ___ The first step to stop coveting is to repent.

5. ___ To keep from coveting, I need to continually thank God for what I do have.

KEY 20
LET PATIENCE WORK

Quote of the Day

"Humility and patience are the surest proofs of the increase of love."
John Wesley

Why is it so difficult for us to wait for what we want? The reason is—patience doesn't come naturally. Galatians 5:17 says, "For the desires of the flesh are against the Spirit, and the desires of the Spirit are against the flesh, for these are opposed to each other, to keep you from doing the things you want to do." We want to be patient, but our flesh does not. It is like a spoiled child who demands to have what he wants immediately. Patience does *not* come naturally; it comes supernaturally. Romans 8:5 says, "For those who live according to the flesh set their minds on the things of the flesh, but those who live according to the Spirit set their minds on the things of the Spirit." (To get a better understanding of this boxing match between the flesh and the spirit, read Romans 5 – 8.)

The devil's two main goals are to keep unbelievers blind and to tempt believers to compromise. II Corinthians 4:4 says, "The god of this world has blinded the minds of unbelievers, to keep them from seeing the light of the gospel of the glory of Christ, who is the image of God." Satan desires to fill the world with darkness so people will not be able to see the light of Christ. His goal is to keep them on the path that leads to death (Proverbs 16:25).

God warns us, as Christians, to be on guard against the schemes of the devil (Ephesians 6:11). Our adversary attempts to deceive us by cloaking his operations in the form of worldly philosophies. (Romans 12:2). His objective is to subtly move us towards a change of allegiance. The devil knows that when we make ourselves friends of the world, we become enemies of God (James 4:4). (He hates human beings because we are all made in the image of the one he hates the most—God.) The following account demonstrates how a worldly philosophy, inspired by the devil, can lead a generation astray.

In the early 1900s, a self-proclaimed New Age prophet and satanist named Aleister Crowley championed an occult philosophy called "Thelema," which effectively divorced God from decision-making, relationships, and the discovery of one's life purpose. The Beatles grabbed hold of this anti-Christ philosophy and used it as the basis of many of their songs. If you doubt this, listen to what John Lennon had to say. In 1966 Lennon claimed, "We're more popular than Jesus now! Christianity will go; it will vanish and shrink."

During the sixty's, America's young people were ripe to receive the message the Beatles brought. Crowley's penchant, "Do what thou wilt!" became the slogan, "Do your own thing!" Our youth turned to an indulgent lifestyle, igniting a culture war that is still raging to this day. At the time of this writing, the truth of God's Word is no longer the standard in our public schools. Even great universities like Harvard have changed their mottos because the vision of their school had changed. Today, public educators tell our young people that God is dead. Immoral behavior is being taught in our schools and libraries. But God has other plans.

God *does* exist. (For an inspiring movie on the existence of God, see "God's Not Dead.") Furthermore, God is *not* out to ruin our fun. He loves all of us very much and wants us to enjoy life to the fullest! He created us with desires—and he loves it when we enjoy his gifts. God wants to fulfill the good ambitions we have, but in *his* way and in *his* timing.

Father God always has our best interest in mind. Every good parent knows that their child cannot have everything they want right when they want it. So, what should we do if we have a desire, but aren't sure about the timing? Go to God in prayer and ask (James 1:5). Here are some questions to ask as you pray:

Is this your best for me? Sometimes we get impulsive, and that can lead to decisions we later regret. Take some time to pray about a decision. Sleep on it. Just give the sand some time to settle before you make the decision. Consider asking a wise friend or relative for some counsel. We all have blind spots, and we need Godly people around us to help us see the things we may not be seeing. Don't be pressured into making an on-the-spot decision.

Is this the right time? Every gift from God has a time. Ecclesiastes 3:1 says, "For everything, there is a season and a time for every matter under heaven." Only Father God knows when it's time for what you want. If you have been desiring something good, then it's likely that you will one day have it. Just don't go after it prematurely. Wait for the right time so you can avoid some undesirable consequences. Trust that Father has your best interest in mind.

What should I do while I wait? Active waiting means we apply effort to our dreams' prerequisites, such as prayer, further study, and discussion. (By the way—sometimes God doesn't tell us what to do next because he's waiting for us to do what he's already told us!)

What are the protective boundaries? Some things are so powerful and precious that they need exceptional care. One example is our sexuality. From God's perspective, sex is not simply a physical act; it's physical and spiritual. It is the bonding of two lives in body and spirit; that's why God has placed protective boundaries around it. According to Scripture, the marriage covenant provides the boundary lines for sexual expression. (For more on this, see "Key 24".)

Remember, patience comes as we set our minds on the things of the Spirit and stay on guard against the schemes of the devil. As we focus on our friendship with Jesus, he will take care of our heart's desires. Psalm 37:4 says, "Delight yourself in the Lord, and he will give you the desires of your heart,"

Meditate on it
Transforming the mind & emotions

My brethren, count it all joy when you fall into various trials, knowing that the testing of your faith produces patience. But let patience have its perfect work, that you may be perfect and complete, lacking nothing.

James 1:2-4 (NKJV)

1. Read it in context: James 1:4 – 8

2. Say it out loud. James 1:2-4

3. Write it out.

_____

_____

_____

_____

_____

_____

4. Pray it: "Lord, I choose to have a good attitude when trials come. Help me to have your perspective during those moments. I trust your timing. As I patiently wait, you will complete all you have in mind for me."

5. Write down your prayer:

_____

_____

_____

_____

_____

_____

_____

_____

Discuss it

Share your thoughts

1. Talk about something for which it is tough to wait.

2. Why is it sometimes difficult to wait for what we want?

3. How has the world's system influenced you?

4. What is one thing you could pray before making an important decision?

Live it

Choose one or more activities, then write what happened

1. Ask for forgiveness for any wrong attitudes during times of waiting.

2. Thank God for what he has already accomplished in your life.

3. Spend time listening to the Holy Spirit, getting his perspective.

4. Ask the Lord what may be blocking a blessing from coming to you.

5. Learn to wait quietly. (Lamentations 3:25-26)

6. Wait eagerly, doing what the Holy Spirit has instructed us to do during the wait. (Galatians 5:5)

7. Sleep on it before making a major decision.

_____

_____

_____

_____

_____

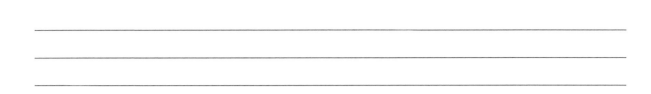

Quiz
True/False

1. ___ Patience comes naturally.

2. ___ The devil's best lies are cloaked in something good.

3. ___ It's always in our best interest to patiently wait for God's timing.

4. ___ God is not interested in my fun.

5. ___ Active waiting may involve applying effort to the prerequisites of your dream.

KEY 21
BREAKTHROUGH IN PRAISE

Quote of the Day

"Praise is the rehearsal of our eternal song, by grace we learn to sing, and in glory we continue to sing."

Charles Spurgeon

As Jesus entered Jerusalem, the multitude of the disciples began praising God so loudly the Pharisees wanted Jesus to rebuke them; but his response was, "I tell you that if these should keep silent, the stones would immediately cry out." (Luke 19:40) All heaven and all creation, especially humans, are specifically designed to praise God. Whether they realize it or not, everyone praises something or someone. Why? Because we are hard-wired to praise! While it is true we don't all praise God—scripture says, in the end, every knee will bow, and every tongue will confess that Jesus is Lord (Philippians 2:10-11). Jesus said, "Love the Lord your God with all your heart, with all your soul, and with all your strength." (Matthew 22:37) Praise happens when we love God with our entire being—our mind, will, emotions, and our physical body.

When we praise God with all of our being:

- We join in with what the angels are already doing in heaven—glorifying God!
- Our spirits are strengthened, which has a profound effect on our hearts and minds.
- We become healthier physically.
- Demons cannot operate. (Psalm 149:6)

- We become more motivated, cooperative, persistent, and hard-working.
- An atmosphere for miracles grows. (God loves to move in power wherever his people are praising.)
- Adverse circumstances lose their effect on us. (Read the story of Paul and Silas in Acts 16:16-34.)

I have a family story to share that shows the power of praise. During our marriage's early days, we had one used car to share and one income–my small teacher's salary. One day we started experiencing some car problems, and our mechanic told us that both the muffler and the clutch of our car needed replacement soon. I came home and gave my wife, Meg, the sad news, then we prayed together that God would intervene. After we prayed, I remembered a book I had read many years earlier called "Power in Praise" by Merlin Carothers. In Acts 16, Paul and Silas praised God in jail while their backs were bleeding. The act of praising God amid their pain released the power of God. There was a violent earthquake, the prison doors flew open, and all the chains fell off the prisoners. Not only that, but the jail-keeper and his household were saved and baptized.

I thought—if it could happen for them, it could happen for us too! I got back into my car to run an errand and, instead of going into fear and doubt, I went into praise. After singing only one word—Jesus—something incredible happened to the car. The noise from the muffler suddenly stopped, and I noticed full power had returned to the car. I was stunned! I got out at a red light to listen to the muffler for just a moment. The noise was gone. As soon as the light turned green, I noticed how well the clutch was working. I began to shake and cry for joy. Glancing down the road, I saw an auto shop, so I stopped in to have them check the car, not telling them what had just happened. The mechanic tested the clutch and the transmission while I held my breath. When he finished, he came over to me and said, "Sir, there is nothing wrong with your car. Your clutch and transmission are fine."

After thanking him with the biggest smile, I headed home to share what had happened with my wife. God had worked a mechanical miracle for us—something I thought only happened on the mission field, but it happened to us—and it happened because of praise amid trial.

Meditate on it
Transforming the mind & emotions

Bless the Lord, O my soul, and all that is within me, bless his holy name! Bless the Lord, O my soul, and forget not all his benefits, who forgives all your iniquity, who heals all your diseases, who redeems your life from the pit, who crowns you with steadfast love and mercy, who satisfies you with good so that your youth is renewed like the eagles.

Psalm 103:2-5

1. Read it in context: Psalm 103
2. Say it out loud. Psalm 103.2-5
3. Write it out:

_____

_____

_____

_____

_____

_____

4. Pray it: "Lord, I praise you with all my heart, soul, mind, and strength! Thank you for all you have done for me—for forgiving all my iniquity, for healing my diseases, for redeeming me, for crowning me with steadfast love and mercy, and for satisfying me with good things and renewing my youth like an eagle."

5. Write down your prayer.

_____

_____

_____

_____

_____

_____

_____

Discuss it
Share your thoughts

1. What does it mean to love the Lord with all your heart, soul, and strength?

2. What good things can happen when we praise God with our entire being?

3. What can you do to go to the next level in praising God?

Live it
Choose one or more activities, then write what happened

1. Open your heart to God and praise him with all your heart. (Speak or sing words of praise out loud.)

2. Thank God for who he is and what he has done.

3. Focus on God's plan for your day.

4. As you sing your praise, think deeply about the words to the song.

5. Use your body to worship. Sing, clap your hands, raise your hands, dance, sing, shout, play an instrument, or just make a joyful noise!

6. Choose to praise even when you don't feel like it.

_____
_____
_____
_____
_____
_____
_____
_____

Quiz
True/False

1. ___ Only religious people praise God.

2. ___ The greatest commandment is to love the Lord with all of our heart, soul, mind, and strength.

3. ___ When we praise God, it creates an atmosphere for miracles.

4. ___ Praise is one of those things we do quietly in our hearts.

5. ___ The Bible says a lot about using the members of our body to praise God.

KEY 22
IGNITE YOUR ZEAL

Quote of the Day

"Do all the good you can, in all the ways you can, to all the souls you can, in every place you can, at all the times you can, with all the zeal you can, as long as ever you can."

John Wesley

Are you zealous for God? Zeal has been called "The blind conductor of the will." It's also referred to in the Bible as fervor. It is the motivating fire in our hearts—it is what gets us up in the morning. According to Webster's 1828 dictionary, zeal is "an eagerness of desire to accomplish or obtain some object." Though God never condones wrong-doing, history shows us he often looks beyond our misbehavior. Father God often focuses more on our potential than he does on our performance.

Of course, it's not a person's raw zeal that God is after in the end; it's the zeal of the Lord. In **Revelation 3:15**, Jesus was imploring the Laodicean church, "I wish you were either cold or hot." Jesus was making a point using their current water problem—lukewarm water. Hot water from the north would be soothing, and cold water from the south would be refreshing, but the lukewarm water they had was useless—even sickening. The Laodiceans were very zealous, but for all the wrong things. Having the zeal of the Lord means we are enthusiastic about the things in God's heart.

Remember, God is not hung up on our past performance because his Son denied Satan the right to hold it against us. Once we receive Father's free gift, his focus is on our new trajectory. He knows the whole course of our lives, and he is committed to getting us there. All it takes is a willingness on our part. Here are some examples from Scripture of ordinary people learned to live in the zeal of the Lord, but may have had a rough start:

- **Noah** was blameless in the midst of an evil generation. Along with his family, he was given the honor of repopulating the earth after it was destroyed by a great flood.
- **Moses** killed an Egyptian, but God chose him to lead Israel's children to the Promised Land.
- **Hannah** was desperate for a child, and God heard her cry and granted her request.
- **David** worshipped God with his whole heart while tending sheep. God made him king.
- **A woman** pushed through the crowd to touch the hem of Jesus' robe–and was instantly healed.
- **Peter** had a will that seemed to be continuously in overdrive. After failing miserably, God restored him and made him one of the greatest of the apostles.
- **Saul** (who became Paul) had quite a bit of misguided zeal. He killed Christians and hauled off others to prison. God used Paul to bring the Gospel to the Gentiles.

What did all these people have in common? They got God's attention because they were in pursuit. Passionate people are exciting to God because zeal is part of his nature. Yes, he loves us all the same—but he does not *use* all of us the same. God, the King, comes looking for a knight to commission for a purpose. II Chronicles 16:9 says, "For the eyes of the Lord range throughout the earth to strengthen those *whose hearts are fully committed to him.*" He's not focused on how good we are, how beautiful we are, how intelligent we are, how well we can speak, or how we feel about ourselves; he's looking at our *hearts*. He is searching for anyone he can find on the earth who will be fully committed to him.

Meditate on it
Transforming the mind & emotions

Do not be slothful in zeal, be fervent in spirit, serve the Lord.

Romans 12:11

1. Read it in context: **Romans 12:9-13**

2. Say it out loud. Romans 12.11

3. Write it out:

_____

_____

_____

_____

_____

_____

4. Pray it: "Father, I will not be slothful in zeal, but fervent in spirit as I continue to serve faithfully."

5. Write down your prayer:

_____

_____

_____

_____

_____

Discuss it
Share your thoughts

1. Describe your zeal for the Lord.

2. In what areas of your spiritual life are you lukewarm?

3. What is the potential for your life God may be focusing on now?

Live it
Choose one or more activities, then write what happened

1. Love God with all your heart, soul, mind, and strength.

2. Look at what Jesus commended in others.

3. Remember your family's heritage.

4. Be faithful with the seemingly small tasks you have been given.

5. Imitate the zeal of those who genuinely follow Christ. (I Corinthians 11:1)

6. Regularly ask for a fresh touch by the Holy Spirit.

_____

_____

_____

_____

_____

Quiz
True/False

1. ___ We can have the zeal of the Lord even if we have made some bad choices in the past.

2. ___ Having the zeal of the Lord means being passionate about the things God is passionate about.

3. ___ God selects those for acts of service who are content with just doing nothing.

4. ___ God looks for those whose hearts are fully committed to him.

5. ___ God recognizes the "small" things you faithfully do unto Him.

KEY 23
ALWAYS FORGIVE

Quote of the Day

"Forgive, forget. Bear with the faults of others as you would have them bear with yours. Be patient and understanding. Life is too short to be vengeful or malicious."
Phillip Brooks

Have you ever stopped to consider just how much God loves you? He wanted a relationship with you so badly that he redeemed you at great cost to himself.

If you haven't already surrendered your life to him, here are the benefits that you can start enjoyed right now:

1. Father accepts you as a member of his own family.
2. You can enjoy fellowship with him.
3. You get to live with him forever.
4. Your heart can be free right now, regardless of your circumstances.

God's heart for us is that we would forgive one another just as he has forgiven us. Colossians 3:12-13 says, "Put on then, as God's chosen ones, holy and beloved, compassionate hearts, kindness, humility, meekness, and patience, bearing with one another and, if one has a complaint against another, *forgiving* each other; as the Lord has forgiven you, so you also must forgive."

What does it mean to forgive? The word "forgive" comes from the old English word "forgiefan," meaning "give, grant, allow, remit, pardon. It means to "give up desire or power to punish." Jesus could have instantly killed the Roman soldiers who had unmercifully tortured him and nailed him to a cross. He could have sent twelve legions of angels, but instead, he prayed, "Father, forgive them, for they know not what they are doing."

We are never more like our heavenly Father than when we act like Jesus—relinquishing our 'right' to punish those who hurt us. During his earthly ministry, Jesus reached out to people with sinful lifestyles, welcoming them and eating with them. He was always eager to forgive the repentant. This infuriated the religious leaders of his day. They muttered, "This man welcomes sinners and eats with them." Jesus knew their thoughts, responding with a parable that contrasted their unforgiving spirit with the extravagant love of his Father. (Luke 15:11-32). The Father in the story represents God, the Father. What is easy to miss is, we are *all* prodigals. Isaiah 53:6 says, "All we like sheep have gone astray; we have turned—everyone—to his own way; and the Lord has laid on him the iniquity of us all." Then there's the elder brother at the end of the story. He typified the religious leaders of Jesus' day and that "holier than thou" attitude that anyone of us can drift into on any given day.

God is a kind, gentle, loving, forgiving father. Justice is not his dominant trait. Jesus said, "Take my yoke upon you, and learn from me, for I am gentle and lowly in heart, and you will find rest for your souls. For my yoke is easy, and my burden is light," (Matthew 11:29-30). If you had a father who constantly criticized you and threatened to punish you for anything you did wrong, would you feel loved by him? Of course not. But that is why some people cannot receive God's love and are unable to forgive. It's because they mistakenly believe that God is exactly like their earthly father, but this is a deception from the enemy, (Genesis 3:5).

Though God cannot excuse our debt of sin, he has provided full payment for it. Jesus took the punishment we deserved for sin over 2,000 years ago. All Father asks of us is that we accept his free gift and surrender our lives to him.

142

Romans 5:1 declares, "Therefore since we have been justified by faith, we have peace with God through our Lord Jesus Christ." When Jesus died on the cross, our sins were nailed there with him. We sometimes think we must do something to make up for the wrongs we have committed (Ephesians 2:8-9), but Jesus has already made full payment on our behalf!

It boils down to this—since God has forgiven us all our sins, how can we withhold forgiveness from those who have wronged us? We can pardon others because God pardoned us. Not to do so is our choice—but the consequences are grave (Matthew 6:15). When we choose not to forgive, we put ourselves above God and thereby consign ourselves to a prison of resentment. When we make daily choices to forgive, we stay free to love.

Have you ever been hurt by someone? Without forgiveness, that pain will not go away. It may seem like it did, but it's just stuffed down inside. Bitterness is a terrible taskmaster. The only way to get free from it is to take it out by the roots. So, when you truly forgive someone from your heart—those bitter roots start coming out. If the person who offended you is a fellow believer, go and share with them how you were hurt (Matthew 18:15-17). If they don't listen, try taking one or two others with you. Don't wait for that person to come to you and ask for forgiveness. It may never happen. You could be consigning yourself to a lifetime of bitterness! Instead, make an all-out effort to forgive them from your heart so that you can be free. It does not mean they are excused from responsibility. No, it releases you from the prison of resentment! If you thought you forgave them, but you are still sensing some bitterness—do it again by faith. Continue asking God to fill you with his love and to help you forgive. Don't give up, and you will be free!

By the way, a potential benefit of forgiveness is that the person who hurt you may now be able to change. Why? Because that's the effect that mercy has on people sometimes; it softens their hearts so that they can turn from their sin. But whether they do or not, you will be free—because you have forgiven.

Meditate on it
Transforming the mind & emotions

Put on then, as God's chosen ones, holy and beloved, compassionate hearts, kindness, humility, meekness, and patience, bearing with one another and, if one has a complaint against another, forgiving each other; as the Lord has forgiven you, so you also must forgive.

Colossians 3:12-13

1. Read it in context: Colossians 3:12-17

2. Say it out loud. Colossians 3:12-13

3. Write it out:

_____

_____

_____

_____

_____

4. Pray it: "**Father,** thank you for loving me. I receive your love again today. Thank you for enabling me to forgive those who have offended me. By your grace, I forgive them now, and I will not hold their sin against them in my heart."

5. Write down your prayer:

_____

_____

_____

_____

_____

_____

_____

Discuss it

Share your thoughts

1. In your own words, what does it mean to forgive?

2. What does the story of the Prodigal Son tell us about Father God?

3. How can Father treat us so kindly when we deserve punishment?

4. Why is it so important to forgive others?

Live it

Choose one or more activities, then write what happened

1. Receive the love of God new every day.

2. Remember how much you've been forgiven.

3. Pray for those who have offended you.

4. Listen to stories of others who have forgiven much

5. Accept God's forgiveness for your sins.

_____

_____

_____

_____

Quiz
True/False

1. ___ Forgiveness means to give up the desire or power to punish.

2. ___ God forgives us our sins, but he'll never forget what we have done.

3. ___ God can forgive us for our sins because Jesus already took our punishment.

4. ___ We can forgive because God has forgiven us.

5. ___ You can only forgive someone if they ask you to forgive them.

KEY 24
KEEP COVENANT

Quote of the Day

"A covenant made with God should be regarded not as restrictive, but as protective."

Russel M. Nelson

God loves us deeply and always has our welfare in mind. **Jeremiah 29:11** says, "For I know the plans I have for you, declares the Lord, plans for welfare and not for evil, to give you a future and a hope." These plans for our welfare begin when we enter a divine partnership—which scripture refers to as a *covenant*. Our covenant with God applies to every area of life—even our finances. **Deuteronomy 8:18** says,

"You shall remember the Lord your God, for it is he who gives you *the power to get wealth*, that he may confirm his covenant that he swore to your fathers, as it is this day."

History clearly shows that societies that embrace God's covenantal ways prosper, and those that reject his ways go into decline. The key, then, to success in life is to do things God's way. It is the Lord who has the answers. His ways are always higher than our ways.

Isaiah 55:8-9 says, "For my thoughts are not your thoughts, neither are your ways my ways, declares the Lord. For as the heavens are higher than the earth, so are my ways higher than your ways and my thoughts than your thoughts."

Here is one example of how God's ways are higher than ours. (When we use the word "covenant" here, we are referring only to biblical covenants.) Many people think in terms of contracts but fail to consider the power of covenant. Let's make a quick comparison between a contract and a covenant:

Contract vs. Covenant

1. Both contracts and covenants begin with a promise between two or more entities.

2. A contract is a legal agreement, but a covenant is a spiritual agreement.

3. A contract can be nullified or voided, but a covenant is perpetual.

4. A contract exchanges one good for another, while a covenant is about giving oneself to another. (Ephesians 5:22-33)

5. The courts enforce a contract, but a Godly covenant is maintained by continued expressions of love, confrontation, and forgiveness. (I Corinthians 7:3-5)

Why does God want to covenant with us?

Father is looking for people who will partner with him as a trusted friend. He wants to love us unconditionally, be there for us in our time of need, share his secrets, and converse with us throughout the day. God also wants to love others through us. How are you doing at loving others? Our care for others is of more concern to Jesus than anything else we could do on earth.

Examples of Covenant

Why are so many believers left disappointed and without joy in their lives? The reason is: they haven't embraced the terms of the covenant they agreed to. They say to themselves, "Well, now

148

that God accepts me, I can do anything I please." This idea is a deception, a lie that the enemy wants us to believe. He doesn't mind at all if we receive Jesus as Savior, then continue in sin, but he does care if we become covenant partners with him.

Here are some examples of covenant:

Baptism

Once you are born again, your next step is baptism. Baptism is your public announcement that you now belong to Christ. Think of it as an engagement ring. It's a sign that you have a brand-new life, that you belong to Christ, and that all your sins are forgiven. Baptism is a covenantal ceremony that announces before witnesses that you have accepted the terms of God's covenant and that you are willing to take upon yourself the name of Christ and keep his commands. In baptism we are saying, "My old life has passed away. When Christ died, my old life died with him and was buried with him. So, I no longer live for myself; I now live for Christ." The terms of that covenant act are simple—we cease to do those evil things connected to our former way of life and begin following the ways of the Lord. We may not do this perfectly, but we choose every day to become more and more like Christ.

Marriage

Like baptism, the marriage covenant is deeply spiritual, symbolizing the union between Christ and his Bride. Every time we see a wedding, we are reminded that Christ will be united with his Church one day. "Then I heard what seemed to be the voice of a great multitude, like the roar of many waters and like the sound of mighty peals of thunder, crying out, "Hallelujah! For the Lord our God, the Almighty reigns. Let us rejoice and exult and give him the glory, for the marriage of the Lamb has come, and his Bride has made herself ready; it was granted her to clothe herself with fine linen, bright and pure—for the fine linen is the righteous deeds of the saints." (Revelation 19:6-8).

Communion

Initially, God instituted this covenantal meal for his people to remember how he delivered them from bondage in Egypt. When Jesus the Messiah came, he concluded his earthly ministry by sharing this same meal with his disciples, but this time it was a celebration of deliverance from sin. Communion reminds us of our forgiveness through the blood of Christ, and also of his life, the bread that we live by every day. It is a corporate covenantal act, a corporate proclamation. I Corinthians 11:23-26 tells us that we share this meal to remember and proclaim what Jesus did for us on the cross. Verse 26 says, "For as often as you eat this bread and drink the cup, you *proclaim* the Lord's death until he comes."

Meditate on it
Transforming the mind & emotions

For the mountains may depart and the hills be removed, but my steadfast love shall not depart from you, and my covenant of peace shall not be removed," says the Lord, who has compassion on you.

Isaiah 54:10

1. Read it in context: Isaiah 54:9-10
2. Say it out loud. Isaiah 54:10
3. Write it out:

_____

_____

_____

_____

150

4. Pray it: Father, thank you that, though terrible things happen in the world, your unfailing love for me will never be shaken, and your covenant of peace with me will not be removed.

5. Write down your prayer:

_____

_____

_____

_____

_____

_____

_____

_____

Discuss it
Share your thoughts

1. What are the differences between a marriage covenant and a marriage contract?

2. Have you been baptized? If so, what does that mean to you now?

3. What is the purpose of taking communion together?

Live it

Choose one or more activities, then write what happened

1. Study the Scriptures to discover God's "terms" for life.

2. Listen to Godly leaders when they admonish you.

3. Always take communion by faith, remembering that it is a sacrament—a spiritual act.

_____

_____

_____

_____

_____

_____

_____

_____

Quiz
True/False

1.___ God makes covenant with us because he has our welfare in mind.

2.___ Baptism is one way we can make covenant with God.

3.___ Covenant is just another word for contract.

4.___ A marriage covenant is the same as a marriage contract.

5.___ Partnering with God means receiving God's love and sharing it with others.

KEY 25
GROW IN GRACE

Quote of the Day

*"Grace is **the** voice that calls us to change and then gives us the power to pull it off."*
Max Lucado

Grace is the favor of God bestowed on the humble in heart. During his earthly ministry, Jesus taught the people what grace was, beginning with this short but powerful statement found in Matthew 5:3, "Blessed are the poor in spirit, for theirs is the Kingdom of Heaven." In other words, favored, happy, and prosperous are the ones who know that they are in desperate need of God—because they have discovered heaven on earth.

It is the grace of God that brings us salvation. It does not depend at all upon our good works. No human being can ever do enough good things to earn God's favor. In the book of Ephesians, Paul writes: For by grace you have been saved through faith. And this is not your own doing; it is the gift of God, not a result of works, so that no one may boast. (Eph. 2:8-9).

We are saved by grace, but we also *live* by grace. Perhaps we feel powerless sometimes because we have become disconnected from our real source and have opted for a pseudo power supply—*ourselves*. God wants us to remember that we cannot do his will in our own strength. Jesus said, "Abide in me, and I in you. As the branch cannot bear fruit by itself, unless it abides in the vine, neither can you, unless you abide in me. I am the vine; you are the branches. Whoever abides in me and I in him, he it is that bears much fruit, for apart from me you can do nothing." (John 15:4-5). God's power activates within us to the extent that we stay connected to Christ. Just as a branch must remain in the tree to receive its life-giving sap, so we must remain in Christ to receive his life. In other words, we cannot go on autopilot. We must stay in a posture of believing, trusting, resting, and receiving the life of Christ.

Apart from him, we can do nothing of any eternal significance, but as we abide in Christ, we can do everything that he has in mind for us, which includes the things we didn't think God cared about: our school grades, relationships, career, finances, and future hopes. As we stay connected to Christ, we receive strength for all of life. As it says in Philippians 4:13, "I can do *all things* through him who strengthens me."

So, what does it mean to "abide" in Christ? First, it means that we are continually receiving from Christ and trusting him. It means we welcome him and stay in fellowship with him. We're talking to him throughout the day and listening to his voice. We are friends. Secondly, it means that we treasure his words. Jesus said, "If you abide in me, and my words abide in you, ask whatever you wish, and it will be done for you." (John 15:7). Putting it another way, when we stay friends with God, cherishing what he says to us, we can ask for anything we wish, and he will do it. That is hard to believe! But think about it. If we were close to God, taking his words seriously, wouldn't we tend to ask for those things that were on his heart?

I want to tell you a story from my own life that illustrates the truth of abiding in Christ. During my elementary years, I suffered from dyslexia, which had a significant impact on my grades. I was always embarrassed about it and was determined to do anything to rid myself of it. When I was in the eighth grade, I attended a week-long Christian seminar that impacted my life. (I enjoyed it so much that I heard the same conference ten more times!) I learned how to apply God's Word to my life in many areas, but what got my attention the most was when the speaker said that his performance in school was subpar in his younger days until he started a particular activity. Once he began this project, his grades soon rose to A's and B's. Now I was excited! I sat up in my seat and listened to him talk about how God's Word can transform our thoughts. He said that there is a difference between just reading the Bible and meditating on it.

The Word must touch our mind, our will, and our emotions. We must go beyond reading it; we must understand it, personalize it, and apply it as well. Here is a verse from Hebrews that describes how powerful the Word is: "For the word of God is living and active, sharper than any two-edged sword, piercing to the division of soul and of spirit, of joints and of marrow, and discerning the thoughts and intentions of the heart." (Hebrews 4:12). Then there's this passage from Psalm 1: Blessed is the man who walks not in the counsel of the wicked, nor stands in the way of sinners, nor sits in the seat of scoffers, but his delight is in the law of the Lord, and on his law, he meditates day and night. He is like a tree planted by streams of water that yields its fruit in its season, and its leaf does not wither. In all that he does, he prospers. (Psalm 1:1-3). So biblical meditation is much more than reading the Bible or even studying it. It's about personalizing it— getting it into the heart. Once it's in the heart, things begin to change!

Getting back to my story—I went home, opened my Bible, pulled out my manual typewriter, and began to find passages of Scripture that I felt were very impacting to me. I studied each portion until I understood the meaning, retyped the verses as personal prayers, and then read those prayers aloud to God regularly. I continued praying the completed prayers aloud, slowly adding more until I had an entire notebook filled with personal meditations.

As a result of this daily practice, my low grades went from C's and D's to mostly A's and a few B's, and I noticed that my dyslexia had vanished! School was no longer so difficult for me. I enjoyed it! It was great not having to struggle through high school. I did so well that I took on advanced English courses and ended up graduating with honors. I decided to go to college, where I received a B.A. and graduated Magna Cum Laude. Of course, my grades were not the only thing that changed; I changed a lot as a person. Much of my shyness, anxiety, and anger dropped off—and my family members started remarking that they could tell I had changed. I felt new inside. I had received grace. As a grade-school teacher in private Christian schools, I made it a point to share this story with my classes to inspire them to do the same.

Meditate on it

Transforming the mind & emotions

Let us then approach God's throne of grace with confidence so that we may receive mercy and find grace to help us in our time of need.

Hebrews 4:16

1. Read it in context: Hebrews 4:14-16
2. Say it aloud. Hebrews 4:16
3. Write it out:

_____

_____

_____

_____

_____

_____

_____

4. Pray it: **Father**, I come before your throne today with confidence because Jesus is my "Great High Priest". I need your help for

_____, so I'm asking for mercy and grace in this time of need.

5. Write **down** your prayer:

_____

_____

_____

_____

_____

_____

_____

_____

_____

_____

Discuss it

Share your thoughts

1. What is grace?

2. What does grace do for us?

3. How do we get more grace?

Live it
Choose one or more activities, then write what happened

1. Continually meditate on God's Word (John 15.7).

2. Come often before the throne in prayer, asking for grace.

3. Focus on the traits that the Spirit produces after salvation: (II Peter 1.5-7): goodness, knowledge, self-control, perseverance, godliness, mutual affection, and love.

4. Grow in dependence on the Holy Spirit as he reveals the truth to you (John 16.13).

5. Grow in obedience and faithfulness to Christ.

_____

_____

_____

_____

_____

_____

_____

_____

_____

_____

Quiz
True/False

1.___ Both grace and works save us.

2.___ Once we are saved, we do good works because we love God and people.

3.___ After we are saved by grace, we then try as hard as we can to please God in our own strength.

4.___ We don't have to ask for more grace because we always have a full supply.

5.___ Grace for each day comes as we abide in Christ.

KEY 26
CONNECT WITH YOUR COMMUNITY

Quote of the Day

Fellowship means, among other things, that we are ready to receive of Christ from others. Other believers minister Christ to me, and I am ready to receive.

Watchman Nee

Ever go to a party and come home feeling empty? That may be because you did not have enough meaningful interaction with others while you were there. Think of this: God himself is a community—Father, Son, and Holy Spirit. He is one God with three distinct members. As human beings, we bear His image, meaning we are much like him. God loves fellowship! He enjoys it so much that he created all of us—not because of loneliness, but because he has such a big heart. Since God has made us in his image, we have that same desire for companionship built into us. He designed us to be together; we are hard-wired for fellowship!

Of course, that's more than just being in the same room together. We have fellowship with other believers to the extent we agree with them, and our focus is on building one another up. As it says in I Corinthians:

"What then, brothers? When you come together, each one has a hymn, a lesson, a revelation, a tongue, or an interpretation. Let all things be done for building up." (I Corinthians 14:25).

Yes, it's vital to spend time alone with God, listening to his voice, and meditating on his Word. But those times are not just for our benefit; they often prepare us for something God would have us share with our fellow believers.

The community of believers is often referred to in the Bible as "The Body of Christ." Pause for a moment and read I Corinthians 12:12-31 to understand how we function together. Here are the main points Paul makes in that passage:

1. There is only *one* Body of Christ. See yourself as a part of something much bigger than yourself. We all need to belong.
2. That one body is made up of many members, each having a different function. It's not one big mouth or even one big hand.
3. Each member should value their place in the body and not wish they had someone else's role. One way to please God is to thank him for how he made you and for the gifts he gave you.
4. The members must not reject the gifts and contributions of their fellow members but honor and care for one another. Be careful not to whisper to others your negative feelings about someone in the body. Do not grieve the Holy Spirit. (Ephesians 4:30)
5. Regardless of who does what in the body, remember that love is the most excellent way. Every gift, every function, and every contribution must come through love. (I Corinthians 13)

Take a moment to evaluate your present level of fellowship. You may be going to church, but are you sharing with others before or after the service? Are you meeting regularly with a small group of believers? If so, do you contribute something? How do you feel after you have shared something encouraging? Most likely, you felt very encouraged—and so did the other members of the group. Often, the things we share are appreciated by others more than we know! If you are not presently in a small group, find one to join or consider starting one.

Meditate on it

Transforming the mind & emotions

Complete my joy by being of the same mind, having the same love, being in full accord, and of one mind. Do nothing from selfish ambition or conceit but in humility count others more significant than yourselves. Let each of you look not only to his own interests, but also to the interests of others.

Hebrews 4:16

1. Read it in context: **Philippians 2:1-4**
2. Say it out loud. **Philippians 2:2-4**
3. Write it out:

_____

_____

_____

_____

_____

_____

_____

_____

_____

4. Pray it
5. Write down your prayer:

_____

_____

_____

_____

Discuss it

Share your thoughts

1. What is your function in the Body of Christ? Why is that valuable?

2. Why do you need to be a part of a small group of believers?

3. How does God's way of love affect the way we use our gifts in the Body?

Live it

Choose one or more activities, then write what happened

1. Find (or start) a small group of like-minded people, such as a group from your home church.

2. Discover your spiritual gifts and use them in the group.

3. Focus on the needs of others.

4. Maintain a personal, intimate relationship with Jesus.

Quiz
True/False

1.___ God created us only for fellowship with himself.

2.___ Fellowship happens when we agree together, and the focus is on building each other up.

3.___ "Building each other up" means being mutually encouraged.

4.___ Some parts of the body are of greater value than other parts.

5.___ One way to cultivate fellowship is by using our spiritual gifts in a small group.

KEY 27
SEE THE BIG PICTURE

Quote of the Day

Where there is no prophetic vision, the people cast off restraint, but blessed is he who keeps the law.

Proverbs 29:18

It is following God's vision for our lives that makes us genuinely happy. God knows the secret to our happiness because he is our Creator. As it says in Proverbs 29.18, "Where there is no prophetic vision, the people are unrestrained, but blessed (happy) is he who keeps the law." Psalm 139 paints that picture for us:

"O Lord, you have searched me and known me! You know when I sit down and when I rise up; you discern my thoughts from afar. You search out my path and my lying down and are acquainted with all my ways. Even before a word is on my tongue, behold, O Lord, you know it altogether. You hem me in, behind and before, and lay your hand upon me. Such knowledge is too wonderful for me; it is high; I cannot attain it." (Psalm 139.1-6)

Since God truly has our highest welfare in mind, and he knows us better than we know ourselves, we can trust his vision for our lives. It is utterly foolish to think we know better than God what the path should be for our lives, and it is equally silly to cast off his restraints. All the benefits God has in mind for us will come into our lives to the extent that we embrace *his* vision for our lives.

At the very beginning, God gave us a mandate. In Genesis, God says to us all: "Be fruitful and multiply and fill the earth and subdue it and have dominion over the fish of the sea and over the birds of the heavens and over every living thing that moves on the earth." (Genesis 1.28)

"The Lord God took the man and put him in the garden of Eden to work it and keep it." (Genesis 2.15)

Then in Isaiah, God speaks about the work that his people will do:
"They shall build up the ancient ruins; they shall raise up the former devastations; they shall repair the ruined cities, the devastations of many generations." (Isaiah 61.4)

All three of these passages talk about the stewardship of the earth and taking care of our cities. Just as good fathers and mothers would have their children take care of their things, so God would have us steward what he has given to us. He wants us to be productive in the work he has called us to do, find ways to multiply that work, and learn how to be self-governed as we work.

The key to productivity is self-government. (All the managers out there said Amen!) Once we yield to God and allow him to give us a new heart, accepting the restraints of God's Spirit becomes less of an obligation and more of a joy. Once we take that first step of obedience through baptism, we are on the road to discipleship—which is the process by which we become more and more like Christ. Every day we get a new opportunity to say "yes" to the Spirit. The more we yield to him, the more we fall in love with him, and the more we love him, the more we get his heart.

As we have said earlier, God's heart is about multiplication. Father desires that all nations would come to know him—that all people would learn his ways and become genuinely blessed as a result. Here's what Jesus said to his disciples just before he ascended to heaven. We call this the Great Commission, which directly connects to the dominion mandate (Genesis 1:26-

168

28.) Jesus said, "Go therefore and make disciples of all nations, baptizing them in the name of the Father and of the Son and of the Holy Spirit, teaching them to observe all that I have commanded you. And behold, I am with you always, to the end of the age." (Matthew 28.19-20*)*

Now let's make this practical. Here are three questions to consider as you prepare yourself to receive God's vision for your life:

1. Are you willing to yield to Christ? Will you allow Him to lead you? Have you submitted to his restraints? Is there an area of your life that is out of control? Take one step this week to restrain that thing by faith.

2. Do you already know what God has called you to do to make a difference in the world? Maybe he wants you to train for a particular occupation. There is no insignificant assignment. Are you open to going in a new direction? If so, do a little research. Ask questions. Pray about it. Find out if that is a good fit for you.

3. Where are you at when it comes to discipleship? Is there someone mature in Christ who would be willing to coach you? Are you currently discipling anyone? If not, who is someone in your life that is open to your input? It does not need to be complicated; just look for opportunities to help someone else achieve Father's vision for their lives.

Meditate on it

Transforming the mind & emotions

His divine power has granted to us everything pertaining to life and godliness through the true knowledge of Him who called us by His own glory and excellence. For by these He has granted to us His precious and magnificent promises, so that by them you may become partakers of the divine nature, having escaped the corruption that is in the world by lust.

II Peter 1:3-4

1. Read it in context: II Peter 1:1-11

2. Say it out loud. II Peter 1:3-4

3. Write it out:

_____

_____

_____

_____

_____

_____

_____

_____

_____

4. Pray it.

5. Write down your prayer:

_____
_____
_____
_____
_____
_____
_____
_____
_____
_____
_____

Discuss it
Share your thoughts

1. Why should you trust God's vision for your life?
2. What is Father God's general vision for humanity?
3. How can you become more self-governed?
4. What does discipleship mean?

Live it
Choose one or more activities, then write what happened

1. Research careers that seem to fit how God has designed you.
2. List a few ways you can become more self-governed. Ask someone to hold you accountable.
3. Evaluate your discipleship. Who would be an ideal mentor for you?
4. How can you multiply who you are and what you do?

Recommended Reading:

- The Hero Maker: Five Essential Practices for Leaders to Multiply Leaders, by Dave Ferguson
- The E Myth Revisited: Why Most Small Businesses Don't Work and What to Do About It, by Michael E. Gerber
- The Purpose Driven Life, by Rick Warren

Quiz
True/False

1. ___ It's following our own vision that makes us genuinely happy.

2. ___ Part of God's vision for our lives is that we help steward the earth.

3. ___ The key to productivity is self-government.

4. ___ The more we love ourselves, the more we get God's heart.

5. ___ The Great Commission is only about getting people saved and baptized.

KEY 28
YIELD TO GOD'S PURPOSES

Quote of the Day

God uses broken things. It takes broken soil to produce a crop, broken clouds to give rain, broken grain to give bread, broken bread to give strength. It is the broken alabaster box that gives forth perfume. It is Peter, weeping bitterly, who returns to greater power than ever.

Vance Havner

Ever wonder why your life seems so frustrating at times? Does it seem like every time you turn around, you are going through another difficulty? Here's an encouraging scripture: "No temptation has overtaken you that is not common to man. God is faithful, and he will not let you be tempted beyond your ability, but with the temptation, he will also provide the way of escape, that you may be able to endure it." (I Corinthians 10:13)

Always remember, God does not want to crush us. No, he wants to release his power from our inner man (our spirit)—and the only way that can happen is through the breaking of our outer man (our mind, will, and emotions). God allows trials to touch our lives to break that hard outer shell. The following passages make it clear that the difficulties we experience in our lives are not wasted moments. Each trial can be turned to gold.

Jesus said, "If anyone would come after me, let him deny himself and take up his cross and follow me. For whoever would save his life will lose it, but whoever loses his life for my sake will find it. (Matthew 16.24-25).

173

The Apostle Paul penned these words: "But we have this treasure in jars of clay, to show that the surpassing power belongs to God and not to us. We are afflicted in every way, but not crushed; perplexed, but not driven to despair; persecuted, but not forsaken; struck down, but not destroyed; always carrying in the body the death of Jesus, so that the life of Jesus may also be manifested in our bodies. . . So, we do not lose heart. Though our outer self is wasting away, our inner self is being renewed day by day. For this light momentary affliction is preparing for us an eternal weight of glory beyond all comparison, as we look not to the things that are seen but to the things that are unseen. For the things that are seen are transient, but the things that are unseen are eternal. (II Corinthians 4:7-10, 16-18).

James, the brother of Jesus, wrote these words in his epistle: "Count it all joy, my brothers, when you meet trials of various kinds, for you know that the testing of your faith produces steadfastness. And let steadfastness have its full effect, that you may be perfect and complete, lacking in nothing." (James 1:2-4).

Finally, we read in Hebrews: "It is for discipline that you have to endure. God is treating you as sons. For what son is there whom his father does not discipline? If you are left without discipline, in which all have participated, then you are illegitimate children and not sons. Besides this, we have had earthly fathers who disciplined us, and we respected them. Shall we not much more be subject to the Father of spirits and live? For they disciplined us for a short time as it seemed best to them, but he disciplines us for our good, that we may share his holiness. For the moment, all discipline seems painful rather than pleasant, but later it yields the peaceful fruit of righteousness to those who have been trained by it." (Hebrews 12:7-11).

Meditate on it

Transforming the mind & emotions

For the moment, all discipline seems painful rather than pleasant, but later it yields the peaceful fruit of righteousness to those who have been trained by it.

Hebrews 12:11

1. Read it in context: Hebrews 12:3-11

2. Say it out loud: Hebrews 12:11

3. Write it out:

_____

_____

_____

_____

_____

_____

_____

_____

_____

_____

4. Pray it.

5. Write down your prayer:

_____

_____

_____

_____

_____

_____

_____

_____

_____

_____

_____

Discuss it
Share your thoughts

1. How can you be sure that God is not out to crush you?

2. Why do you think people get angry with God when bad things happen to them?

3. How does God transform us through trials?

4. According to Scripture, what should be your response when you encounter difficulty in life?

Live it
Choose one or more activities, then write what happened

1. Present yourself daily to God as a "living sacrifice" (Romans 12.1)

2. Ask the question, "What do you see in me that needs to go to the cross?"

3. Be willing (and comfortable with) being wrong.

4. See trials as blessings and rejoice in them. (James 1.3)

5. Let go of control, allowing God to accomplish a thing in his time.

6. Thank someone for a compliment without asking for more.

7. Release an expectation to God.

_____

_____

_____

_____

_____

_____

_____

_____

_____

Quiz
True/False

1.___ We need only surrender to God once in our lives.

2.___ God permits trials so that we will be broken, releasing the treasure inside.

3.___ All that is necessary as we walk with Christ is to be broken.

4.___ The Lord's discipline is always pleasant.

5.___ We can cultivate brokenness by rejoicing in our trials.

KEY 29
RESPECT AUTHORITY

Quote of the Day

When we treat people merely as they are, they will remain as they are. When we treat them as if they were what they should be, they will become what they should be.

Thomas S. Monson

Do you sometimes wish you could get just a bit more respect? Here's how Jesus said it works, "So whatever you wish that others would do to you, do also to them, for this is the Law and the Prophets." We can apply this life principle in many ways. For example: If you want to have friends, be friendly. If you'd appreciate some kindness, then be kind to others. If you would like to be respected, show respect, especially to those who hold positions of authority.

"You have heard that it was said, 'You shall love your neighbor and hate your enemy.' But I say to you, love your enemies and pray for those who persecute you, so that you may be sons of your Father who is in heaven. He makes his sun rise on the evil and on the good and sends rain on the just and on the unjust. For if you love those who love you, what reward do you have?" *(Matthew 5.43-46)*.

In the natural, it's so easy to react when someone in authority has wronged us. But what do we gain by treating them the same way they treated us? Nothing. And what did that authority receive that could help them make a good change? Nothing. So, the phrase "Love your

179

enemies" means we need to love the leaders we don't like? Yes, it does. Remember the words of Jesus, "Do not be overcome by evil, but overcome evil with good." (Romans 12.21**.)**

So, showing disrespect to authority is not productive for us *or* the one in charge. In fact, Scripture says resisting authority puts us at odds with God. (Remember that in this context, we are not talking about domestic violence or removing evil dictators from power. That falls under a different category that is not being addressed here.) "Let every person be subject to the governing authorities. For there is no authority except from God, and those that exist have been instituted by God. Therefore, whoever resists the authorities resists what God has appointed, and those who resist will incur judgment." (Romans 13:1-2).

One question that is often asked is, "What do I do if someone in leadership asks me to do something I know is wrong? The Bible is full of stories like this. Just because someone is in leadership doesn't mean we should follow any instruction they may give. Every decision must be seen through the lens of God's Word. There is often a way to show respect to authority and obey God's Word at the same time. It's called making a respectful appeal. For an example of that, read Daniel 1:8-16.

Now let's look at the positive side. Honoring authority, even those who are unkind, brings us great rewards. Remember, respecting authority does *not* include obeying them when they ask us to do something wrong. It also doesn't mean we ignore their bad behavior. Honor is not rubber-stamping a leader's policies and behavior; instead, it releases the Holy Spirit to do the miraculous. We honor someone's position of authority for our protection and benefit. In Ephesians 6:2-3, God gives us this promise, "Honor your father and mother (this is the first commandment with a promise,) that it may go well with you and that you may live long in the land." In other words, if you want it to go well for you and live a long life, honor authority.

Here's a story from our lives that will help illustrate this principle further. When I was getting to know Meg before we were married, I asked her if she would like to go with me to see a stage production of "Fiddler on the Roof." Her response surprised me. She said, "You'll need to ask my Dad first." I was so excited! Meg was the kind of person I had been waiting to meet, one who understood the principle of honoring authority. I gladly gave her dad a call. Meg didn't let him know that I would be calling, but when I asked him for permission to take her to the play, he simply responded, "Sure! Have a good time." That was it! When I put the phone down, I thought, "Well, that was easy." Little did I know just how much that phone call meant to Meg's dad. It so impressed him that I would ask for his consent that he quickly responded with a "yes" when I later asked permission to marry his daughter. This act set the stage for a good relationship with our in-laws for years to come. The point is, a simple act of respect can easily lead to another, resulting in an ongoing relationship of mutual respect.

Other scriptures on this topic:

Titus 3.1; I Timothy 2.1-2; I Peter 2.13; Romans 13.5; Hebrews 13.7

Recommended Reading:

"Under Cover," by John Bevere

Meditate on it

Transforming the mind & emotions

We ask you, brothers, to respect those who labor among you and are over you in the Lord and admonish you.

I Thessalonians 5:12

1. Read it in context: I Thessalonians 5:12-13
2. Say it out loud: I Thessalonians 5:12

3. Write it out:

_____

_____

_____

_____

_____

_____

_____

_____

4. Pray it.

Write down your prayer:

_____

_____

_____

_____

_____

_____

_____

_____

_____

_____

Discuss it
Share your thoughts

1. What's the best way to earn more respect?
2. According to Ephesians 6, what are the rewards of honoring parents?
3. What do I do if I have dishonored my parents?
4. How else can I honor authority?
5. What if a leader asks me to do something morally wrong?
6. Why does a suitor need to ask permission of the father?

Live it
Choose one or more activities, then write what happened

1. Listen carefully to the stories and opinions of *all* people.
2. Honor your parents regardless of their past performance.
3. Love your enemies (Matthew 5:44).
4. Give special honor to those who have laid down their lives for our country.
5. Do your part to steward the environment.
6. Do all you can to protect all life, including the unborn.
7. Regularly give to charitable organizations, especially your local church.

Quiz
True/False

1.___ The golden rule says, "Do to others whatever they do to you."

2.___ Scripture teaches that we should honor parents only when they deserve to be honored.

3.___ Jesus demonstrated for us how to live as one who has delegated authority.

4.___ Scripture teaches that we are to esteem those who are in authority over us in the Lord.

5.___ Respecting authority does not mean breaking the law if asked to do so.

KEY 30
LOVE, NO MATTER WHAT

Quote of the Day

In the New Testament, love is more of a verb than a noun. It has more to do with acting than with feeling. The call to love is not so much a call to a certain state of feeling as it is to a quality of action.

R.C. Sproul

Of all the gifts God has given us, the greatest is love (I Corinthians 13:13). Scripture says God himself *is* love (I John 4:8). This means that when God shares love with us, he shares himself! How does this happen? Let's discuss two critical insights into the love of God:

First, God's love is not earned; it is received. Throughout human history, humanity has struggled with guilt over sin. We desire acceptance by God, so we busy ourselves with trying to earn his approval. Father's perspective is different. He knows that no one, except his Son, can be good enough—so he sent Jesus as his perfect expression of love to us. John writes,

"In this the love of God was made manifest among us, that God sent his only Son into the world so that we might live through him. In this is love, not that we loved God but that he loved us and sent his Son to be the expiation for our sins. *(I John 4:9-21)*

Jesus didn't come to earth to die for us because we *deserved* his love. No, he proved the extent of his love by giving his life for us while we were still sinners. As it says in Romans 5:8, "While we were still sinners, Christ died for us." So, though we do nothing to earn God's love, we do need to be *willing* to receive it. God chooses not to violate our free will because that would not be in harmony with his nature.

185

He doesn't force his love upon us, for, in that case, it would cease to be love. Instead, he repeatedly broadcasts his love to us and waits for us to receive it. The world we live in is filled with illustrations of this: a quarterback looks downfield, waiting for a receiver, radio waves go out, but only radios that are turned on receive the signal, a Christmas present is appreciated because it is received by an excited loved one.

Think for a moment about how much God loves you! He is intimately acquainted with you. (Psalm 139) He knows your every thought. Even the hairs on your head are all numbered (Matthew 10:30.) He has a purpose for your life, which perfectly matches the your design. You are no accident! God had you in his mind before you were born. His book records every one of your days. As it says in Psalm 139:15-18, "My frame was not hidden from you, when I was being made in secret, intricately woven in the depths of the earth. Your eyes saw my unformed substance; in your book were written, every one of them, the days that were formed for me, when as yet there was none of them. How precious to me are your thoughts, O God! How vast is the sum of them! If I would count them, they are more than the sand. I awake, and I am still with you."

When we were born again, we received God's gift of love for the first time, and now we have the choice to accept it again and again—every day! So, let's review. The first thing we understand about God's love is: It is not earned but received.

The second thing we learn about God's love is that it must be reciprocated. God's love is not complete until it has made its circuit from God to us, then from us to one another. God is continually pouring in, but we must be continuously pouring out. If the life of God comes to us, but we are not, in turn, giving it out, then we become like the Dead Sea. Besides, if it is all one way, then it is no longer a relationship. Father has always wanted a love *relationship* with us, where he leads the dance, and we respond. Listen to the heart of God expressed to us in I John:

"Beloved, if God so loved us, we also ought to love one another. No man has ever seen God; if we love one another, God abides in us, and his love is perfected in us. By this, we know that we abide in him and he in us, because he has given us of his own Spirit. And we have seen and testify that the Father has sent his Son as the Savior of the world. Whoever confesses that Jesus is the Son of God, God abides in him, and he in God. So, we know and believe the love God has for us. God is love, and he who abides in love abides in God, and God abides in him. . . We love because he first loved us. If anyone says, "I love God," and hates his brother, he is a liar; for he who does not love his brother whom he has seen, cannot love God whom he has not seen. And this commandment we have from him, that he who loves God should love his brother also." *(*I John 4.11-21). We respond to God's love by loving him in return, keeping his commands. Jesus said to his disciples, "If you love me, you will keep my commandments." *(*John 14.15).

We cannot say that we love God if we don't do what he says. Love and obedience go together – hand and glove. Imagine a child saying to his mother, "I love you, mom," then disobeying what she said to do. Would that mother feel loved in that instance? Of course not! It's the same way with God. He loves to hear the words, "I love you," but he desires to see the substance of that confession—which is obedience to his Word.

As you read the New Testament, record how many times God encourages his people to love one another. Why do we need to be told so many times? It's because we all tend to revert to old patterns of behavior. Our natural man prefers to love itself. No one needs to teach a child to be selfish. That is their natural state! We need to encourage ourselves to give selflessly to others every day.

Do you sometimes worry that God will change his mind about you? No, he never will! As it says in Romans 8:31-39, "Who shall separate us from the love of Christ? Shall tribulation, or distress, or persecution, or famine, or nakedness, or peril, or sword? For I am sure that neither death, nor life, nor angels, nor principalities, nor things present, nor things to come, nor powers, nor height, nor depth, nor anything else in all creation, will be able to separate us from the love of God in Christ Jesus our Lord."

In this course you have delved into many Kingdom principles, but they only work through God's love. Without Father's love in our hearts, spiritual gifts mean nothing, faith means nothing, and even self-sacrifice means nothing. Nothing counts unless it is born out of the love of God in our hearts. I Corinthians 13:1-3 says, "If I speak in the tongues of men and of angels, but have not love, I am a noisy gong or a clanging cymbal. And if I have prophetic powers, and understand all mysteries and all knowledge, and if I have all faith, so as to remove mountains, but have not love, I am nothing. If I give away all I have, and if I deliver up my body to be burned, but have not love, I gain nothing."

The question then remains—how do I get more of the love of God? We find true love only in Christ. Jesus said, "Without me, you can do nothing." If we want to know how to love better, we must come to know God better—because God is love. Jesus is the personification of love on the earth. Think about the character of Christ as you read this passage from I Corinthians 13:4-7:

"Love is patient and kind; love is not jealous or boastful; it is not arrogant or rude. Love does not insist on its own way; it is not irritable or resentful; it does not rejoice at wrong but rejoices in the right. Love bears all things, believes all things, hopes all things, endures all things."

Now let's personalize the passage:

- Christ in me is patient and kind.
- Christ in me does not envy or boast.
- Christ in me is not arrogant or rude.
- Christ in me does not insist on having its way.
- Christ in me is not irritable or resentful.
- Christ in me does not rejoice at wrongdoing but rejoices with the truth.
- Christ in me bears all things, believes all things, hopes all things, and endures all things.

How do we walk out a life of love? It begins by focusing our minds on the things of the Spirit. Romans 8:5 declares, "For those who live according to the flesh set their minds on the things of the flesh, but those who live according to the Spirit set their minds on the things of the Spirit. For to set the mind on the flesh is death, but to set the mind on the Spirit is life and peace."

In our friendship with God, we learn to set our minds on God's thoughts. It is a day-by-day, moment-by-moment dependence upon the Holy Spirit. It is all about overflow. As we stay connected to him, he fills us with his love again and again so that we have a surplus of His love to share with others.

Meditate on it
Transforming the mind & emotions

Whoever has my commandments and keeps them, he it is who loves me. And he who loves me will be loved by my Father, and I will love him and manifest myself to him."

John 14:21

1. Read it in context: John 14:18-24
2. Say it out loud: John 14:21
3. Write it out:

_____

_____

_____

_____

_____

_____

_____

_____

4. Pray it.

Write down your prayer:

_____

_____

_____

_____

_____

_____

_____

_____

_____

Discuss it
Share your thoughts

1. Do you feel loved by God? Why do you feel that way?

2. What scripture explains how God feels about you?

3. How do you know that you love God?

4. How can you get more of the love of God?

Live it

Choose one or more activities, then write what happened

1. Take simple steps of obedience, following through on things that God has already made clear.

2. "Seek *first* the Kingdom," not just your own needs and desires.

3. Lay down your life for your friends. (John 15.13)

4. Study the life of Jesus and imitate the way he lived.

5. Maintain a close friendship with God, listening to his voice and receiving his love.

6. Write a list of ways you could practically love the people in your life, then decide to do one of those each day.

Quiz

True/False

1.___ Love is primarily a feeling.

2.___ The best way to learn how to love better is to know God better.

3.___ God supplies all my needs as I put his Kingdom and his righteousness first.

4.___ We know we love God primarily because we feel it inside.

5.___ We cultivate love by listening to Father's voice and receiving his love.

Quiz Key & Scores

	Answers	# Correct	Notes (areas to restudy, etc.)
1	T, F, F, T, T		
2	T, F, F, T, T		
3	T, T, F, F, F		
4	T, F, T, T, T		
5	F, T, T, T, F		
6	F, T, F, T, T		
7	T, T, F, T, F		
8	F, T, F, T, T		
9	F, T, F, F, T		
10	F, T, T, F, T		
11	T, T, T, F, T		
12	F, T, T, F, T		
13	F, F, T, F, T		
14	T, F, F, T, T		
15	T, F, F, T, T		
16	F, T, F, F, F		
17	T, F, T, F, T		
18	F, F, T, T, T		
19	F, T, F, T, T		
20	F, T, T, F, T		
21	F, T, T, F, T		
22	T, T, F, T, T		
23	T, F, T, T, F		
24	T, T, F, F, T		
25	F, T, F, F, T		
26	F, T, T, F, T		
27	F, T, T, F, F		
28	F, T, F, F, T		
29	F, F, T, T, T		
30	F, T, T, F, T		
	Grand Total:		
	Final %:		(Divide your total correct by 150)

ABOUT THE AUTHOR

John Hart has spent his entire career in the field of education. He has a passion for imparting God's truth. John is also a gifted pianist and composer. One of his many songs, "Great is Your Love," was published by Integrity Music in 1986 and is still sung in churches around the world today. John is the model of a Godly man. The power behind his ministry stems from his close walk with Jesus. You can find John's piano music, worship songs, and Scripture meditations online by searching YouTube for John Wesley Hart.

John and Meg have raised five children and have twelve grandchildren at the time of this writing. Pastors and other leaders have encouraged them to share the biblical principles of success they walk in. "Together, John and Meg are a fine example that other marriages can tune up to. Their passion is discipling young adults who are hungry to know God and build strong families." John and Meg attend Camano Chapel in Washington State.

Made in United States
Troutdale, OR
01/10/2024

16829315R00113